SKYE

SKYE

ANN MACSWEEN

PHOTOGRAPHS BY JOHN COOPER

CANONGATE

For Ian

ACKNOWLEDGEMENTS

SINCE I began researching this book three or four years ago many people have volunteered information, pointed me in the right direction and discussed my ideas with me. My grateful thanks are due to Murdo and Mary Campbell; Andrew Currie, Nature Conservancy Council Representative for Skye; Liz Murphy of the Highlands and Islands Development Board, Inverness; George and Sandy Kozikowski; Ronnie and Chrissie MacSween; Roddie and Patsy MacPherson; Roger Miket, Skye Museums Officer; the Staff of the National Library, Edinburgh, especially Ruzena Wood of the Music Department; Tessa Ransford, Director of the Scottish Poetry Library, Edinburgh; Mick Sharp and Jean Williamson; and Grace and Paul Yoxon, Broadford Field Centre.

Several people deserve a particular thankyou, as they have seen the book through all its stages, encouraging and threatening me as necessary. They are my parents John and Rhoda MacSween, my brother Ian MacSween and my husband Jim Killgore. I am grateful to my mother for her help with the Gaelic and for translating the extracts from 'An Gleann 's an robh mi òg' and 'Eilean a' Cheo' and to Jim for editing my text and smoothing out many of the rough edges.

My thanks also to: Penguin books for permission to print the extract from *Harpoon at a Venture*; Aoengus MacNeacail and Macdonald Publishers for permission to reproduce 'Going Home 2'; Miss Lucy Sanderson Taylor for allowing me to quote her poem 'These Quiet Stones'; and Routledge and Kegan Paul for permission to quote 'The Men have gone to Scavaig'. The lyrics for 'Skye' by C. MacDonald and R. MacDonald Copyright © 1988 were reproduced by kind permission of Chrysalis Music.

Finally, John and I would like to thank the staff at Canongate for their support throughout the project.

Ann MacSween, April 1990

First published in Great Britain in 1990
by Canongate Publishing Ltd, Edinburgh

Copyright text © Ann MacSween 1990
Copyright photographs © John Cooper 1990

Designed by Dorothy Steedman

British Library Cataloguing in Publication Data
MacSween, Ann
Skye.
1. Scotland. Highland Region. Skye
I. Title
941.182

ISBN 0-86241-289-7

Typeset by Advanced Filmsetters (Glasgow) Ltd
Printed and bound by Butler & Tanner Ltd, Frome

Overleaf:
Raasay from
Sconser

CONTENTS

EILEAN TRODDAY

RUBHA HUNISH

SCORE BAY

SHVLISTA
DUNTULM
KILMALUAG
CONNISTA
FLODIGARRY
HUNGLADER
KILMUIR
QUIRAING
MONKSTADT

KILMALUAG BAY

STAFFIN BAY
STAFFIN
KILT ROCK

SKUDIBURG

UIG

UIG BAY

BEINN EDRA

TROTTERNISH

VATERNISH POINT

ASCRIB ISLANDS

TRUMPAN

ARDMORE POINT

ISAY ISLAND

VATERNISH

KINGSBURGH

RIGG

DUNVEGAN HEAD

LOCH BAY
STEIN
BAY
CLAGGAN

LOCH GRESHORNISH

LYNDALE
BERNISDALE
EDINBANE

LOCH SNIZORT BEAG

EYRE

THE STORR

BEARRERAIG BAY

LOCH POOL TEIL

BORERAIG

LOCH DUNVEGAN

FAIRY BRIDGE

LOCH LEATHAN

LOCH FADA

GLENDALE
COLBOST
WATERSTEIN

DUNVEGAN
UIGINISH

SKEABOST

NEIST POINT

DUIRINISH

ACHTALEAN

PORTREE

BROCHEL CAS.

RAMASAIG

MACLEOD'S TABLE

ROAG
ORBOST

VATTEN

S
K
Y
E

BRAES

CAMASTIANAVAIG

RAASAY

LORGILL

OSDALE

SOUND OF RAASAY

LOCH CAROY

BRACADALE

STRUANMORE

LOCH BRACADALE

WIAY

IDRIGILL POINT

LOCH HARPORT

BEN LEE

LONGAY

PORTNALONG

CARBOST

TALISKER BAY

TALISKER

DRYNOCH

LOCH SLIGACHAN

GLAMAIG

SLIGACHAN

SCALPAY

PABAY

KYLE MORE

LOCH AINORT

EYNORT

MINGINISH

LOCH EYNORT

CUILLIN HILLS

LOCH CORUISK

BLAVEN

RED HILLS

TORRIN

BEINN NA CAILLICH

CORRY

ARSHAIG

BROADFORD

KYLE

KYLEAKIN

KYLERHEA

GLENBRITTLE

KILBRIDE
KILCHRIST

RUDH AN DUNAIN

SUISNISH

BORERAIG

KINLOCH

LOCH BRITTLE

SOAY SOUND

SOAY

LOCH SCAVAIG

ELGOL

GLASNAKILLE

LOCH SLAPIN

LOCH EISHORT

ORD
TOKAVAIG
DUNSCAITH
CASTLE

KNOCK

SOUND OF SLEAT

ISLEORNSAY

SLEAT

KILMORE

ARMADALE

POINT OF SLEAT

MALLAIG

INTRODUCTION

MRS Sarah Murray was not one to let fashion get in the way of practicalities. She was a stout, hearty woman, and on this day, 5th August 1800, she wore a large shapeless beaver-skin hat, fastened securely under her chin with a thick ribbon. The ribbon was to prevent the hat from being blown off by the squalls which buffeted the small open boat in which she was sailing from Rhum to Skye. From the relative safety of the bottom of the boat she experienced with awe her first sight of the Cuillin Hills, while keeping an eye out for the swinging gib, as the boat approached Loch Eynort.

In her sixtieth year Mrs Murray was making a journey which few men, far less women, had undertaken. Her purpose was to write a book on travel to the Western Isles, one which she hoped would be of practical use to other visitors. Skye in the early nineteenth century was an inhospitable place for travellers. There were few inns, and where roads existed at all they were rough tracks. Mrs Murray sensibly left her carriage on the mainland.

From Loch Eynort she planned to travel overland to Talisker. Only one horse was available, which she had to share with her escort Revd MacLean, her guide, Angus, walking behind.

> Fortunately the day was fair, so I accomplished the distance of 9 or 10 miles without much fatigue, although it took above seven hours to do it. The road from the head of Loch Eynort to Talisker is extremely bad, up and down rough precipices; and what added to our distress, there was no such thing as obliging the horse to go on the road, because having no shoes on, he would scramble to every patch of green to save his feet, and avoid the stones in the track. I almost strangled Mr MacLean by holding his coat so tightly, in order to keep myself on behind him, and Angus walked at the tail of the horse to catch me, in case I slipped off, which happened every now and then, so that it was a continual petition on my part 'Oh! Angus help me'; and, 'Oh! Mr MacLean, stop and take me up, for I am tired with walking'.

Mrs Murray's book was one of the first to express an appreciation for the beauty of Skye, for the type of scenery that travellers once thought could only be seen in the Alps. Although a variety of people had written books on the Hebrides from personal experience, she was the first to produce a proper travel guide.

Skye is the largest of the Inner Hebrides which lie off the north-west coast of Scotland. Although forty-eight miles from north to south, and twenty-seven from east to west at its widest point, Skye's jagged coastline ensures that no point is more than five miles from the sea.

The island is ringed with smaller islands and skerries, the largest being Raasay to the east which, along with Scalpay, Pabay and Longay, forms a barrier between Skye and the mainland. Timothy Pont produced the first map of Skye in 1654. Somehow the southernmost peninsula, Sleat, was missed off the map completely.

The earliest description of Skye from firsthand observation was by Dean Munro, writing in 1549 –

> The iyle is callit by the Erishe, Ellan Skyane, that is to say in English, the Wingitt ile, be reason it has maney wings and points lyand furth frae it through the devyding of thir lochs.

It is possible that 'Skye' is a derivation of 'Sgiath', the Norwegian for 'wing', but another theory is that the island's name derived from the Norwegian word 'Ski', meaning a mist, hence the sobriquet 'The Misty Isle'.

The first detailed account of the natural history and people of Skye was given by Martin Martin, who wrote about the Hebrides in the early eighteenth century. Martin's observations were wide-ranging, covering subjects fom local cures for jaundice to how to catch a young whale. A Skyeman, he seemed to have little appreciation of the bleak and rugged scenery of his homeland and did not think it worthy of mention.

Likewise, travellers like the naturalist Thomas Pennant who visited Skye in 1772, and the London literary figure Samuel Johnson and his lawyer companion James Boswell, who visited the island a year later, took little notice of the dramatic seascapes or the Cuillin Hills. Pennant described the Cuillin Hills as 'a savage series of mountain', while Johnson complained that 'a walk upon ploughed fields in England is a dance upon carpets compared to the toilsome drudgery of wandering in Skye'.

It was not until after Mrs Murray's time that Highland scenery became fashionable. The 'romanticisation' of the Highlands was due largely to the writings of Sir Walter Scott, who found a beauty in the bareness. Lord Cockburn, who travelled to Skye in 1841, described his view of the area around Broadford approached from Kylerhea – '. . . all below is beautiful. Perfectly treeless, hard looking, and bare, but still capable of all the beauty that a bright sun can bestow on calm water, and on silent massive hills.' Artists such as the engraver William Daniell and the painter William Turner were among the first to commit their impressions of the wildness of Loch Coruisk and the Cuillin Hills to canvas. Turner's painting of the Cuillin Hills is a dramatic mist-swathed view of Loch Coruisk.

Other early travellers came to climb Skye's formidable Cuillin Hills, the mountains which dominate the island's profile. Sixteen summits of the main Cuillin Ridge attain heights of over 3,000 ft. In the 1810s the geologist John MacCulloch tried to climb the Cuillin Hills seven times in five successive visits, but failed. He blamed the weather, but the more likely explanation is that the ascents were attempted on horseback.

One of the first to scramble in the Cuillin Hills was the Revd Lesingham Smith, a Fellow of Christ's College, Cambridge. He visited Skye in 1835 and stayed at Sligachan for part of the time. One day, with a forester as a guide, he visited Loch Coruisk, and on the return the pair took a short-cut over the Cuillin Hills, directly over the ridge at the head of Loch Coruisk. At the more difficult parts, Lesingham Smith pushed the forester up, and was then pulled up in return. During the climb Lesingham Smith found his umbrella 'a sad nuisance'.

Although the earliest recorded ascent of the Black Cuillins was made in 1836 by the geologist and physicist James Forbes when he climbed Sgurr nan Gillean, Sheriff Alexander Nicolson of Skye was the first to explore the Cuillin Hills extensively. Sgurr Alasdair, the highest peak in the range (3,251 ft) is named after Nicolson who scaled the mountain in 1873.

The Red Hills, the other major mountain range in the south of the island, have more rounded profiles. One of the most impressive peaks is Beinn na Caillich, the Hill of the Old Woman. The old woman is said to be one 'Saucy Mary', who stretched a chain between Kyle and Kyleakin to exact tolls from boats sailing through the sound. Another of the peaks, Glamaig, was ascended in 1899 by a Gurkha soldier Havildar Harkabir Thapa who ran from the old bridge at Sligachan to the top of the 2,542 ft high mountain in thirty-seven minutes, and back down in eighteen minutes, in bare feet.

Marsco and Glen Sligachan

Portree Bay

The increased interest in visiting Skye in the mid-nineteenth century was due in part to improvements in transport. By 1840 the island had a weekly steamship service between Glasgow and Portree. Prior to this, travel by sailing ship could take between ten and fifteen days.

The only alternative was a difficult overland coachride. Mrs Sarah Murray was experienced at the hardships of this mode of travel. Her book *A Companion and Useful Guide to the Beauties of Scotland* included some practical advice on outfitting a coach for such a journey –

> Provide yourself with a strong roomy carriage, and have the springs well corded; have also a stop-pole and strong chain to the chaise. Take with you linch-pins, and four shackles, which hold up the braces of the body of the carriage; a turn-screw, fit for fastening the nuts belonging to the shackles; a hammer, and some straps. For the inside of the carriage, get a light flat box, the corners must be taken off, next the doors, for the more conveniently getting in and out. This box should hang on the front of the chaise, instead of the pocket . . . the side next the travellers should fall down by hinges, at the height of their knees, to form a table on their laps; the part of the box below the hinges should be divided into holes for wine bottles to stand upright in. The part above the bottles to hold tea, sugar, bread, and meat; a tumbler glass, knife and fork, and salt-cellar, with two or three napkins: the box to have a very good lock. I would also advise to be taken, bed-linen, and half a dozen towels at least, a blanket, thin quilt, and two pillows . . .

Even once Skye was in sight, getting a carriage across the short stretch of sea could also pose problems, as Lord Cockburn found out in 1841 when he endeavoured to take his coach by ferry from the Mainland to Kylerhea.

> This ferry, though boasted as the best in Skye, is detestable, at least for carriages, and is as ill-conducted as possible. But what can a ferry be for carriages, where ours is only the third that has passed this year, and the object of the landlord of the ferry-house on each side is to detain instead of advancing the passenger, and where, when at last it is seen that they can carry it on no longer, the only machinery for putting the vehicle on board consists of dozens of lazy and very awkward Highlanders, all scolding in Erse, who almost lift it and throw it into the groaning boat.

In 1897 a ten and a half mile stretch of railway linked Kyle to the West Highland Line, making the journey to Skye immeasurably easier. The line still operates today.

Weather was a common complaint of the early travellers, as it often is with today's visitors. Lesingham Smith complained that while rambling in the Cuillin Hills, 'Boisterous gusts of wind swept fitfully past us, as we penetrated farther and farther; then an occasional shower; and at last the genuine Highland storm burst on us with all its fury. If any one desire to learn how thick and fast rain can fall, let him witness a tempest in the midst of the Cuillins.'

Johnson said of the Skye weather – '[It] is not pleasing. Half the year is deluged with rain. From the autumnal to the vernal equinox, a dry day is hardly known, except when the showers are suspended by a tempest'. Perhaps Johnson exaggerates, but it is true that Skye's oceanic climate produces, on average, fifty to sixty inches of rain a year, double the rainfall of Edinburgh. The highest parts of the Cuillin Hills average more than double even this amount. And then there are the westerly gales which frequently buffet the west coast. However, the temperature is mild, and there is a low frequency of frost and snow.

The Outer Isles ferry leaving Uig Bay

The travel writer 'Nauticus' who journeyed round the island as part of a two and a half thousand mile trip around Scotland, had little good to say about Skye's weather. Nauticus travelled by tricycle, a Cheylesmore. Not surprisingly, the journey was arduous. One of the most difficult stretches of road for him was the Bealach Udal between Kyleakin and Broadford. Nauticus noted in his account of the trip that 'the gradient was such as to make me fear that I should have to take my tricycle to pieces and carry it up bit by bit'. Going down the other side was just as traumatic. The wind was so strong behind him that he built up a frightening speed and was afraid to brake in case he caused 'a double somersault into the yawning abyss'.

Today most travellers arrive on Skye by car, sailing from the Kyle of Lochalsh to Kyleakin on a ten minute ferry crossing. A journey from Edinburgh which would have taken days by carriage can be accomplished in less than six hours.

Skye's main roads tend to hug the coastal outline, much of the island's rugged interior still accessible only on foot. Settlement tends to be limited to the gentler and more fertile coastal slopes.

Many of Skye's visitors arrive by tourist bus and after a quick tour of the island are deposited in Portree, the unofficial capital of Skye. Here they shop for souvenirs in this picturesque town built on the hillsides and cliffs surrounding a small bay.

Travel to Skye is now easy, perhaps too easy in some people's opinion. The proposed bridge link with the mainland would take away even the prospect of a sea journey. Certainly a measure of anticipation, of excitement, will be lost, that same excitement felt by Mrs Sarah Murray clutching her beaver-skin hat on a blustery day in 1800.

Ruined castle near Tokavaig

Shed, Waterstein

Rock Pools

NORTHWARD

Under a hillside by sunny Gareloch,
Scaring the cormorant off his wave-perch, floated
Forth on the springtime into my element
I, the yacht Northward.

Seven brothers built my body of oak and elm,
Woke in the dumb wood a spirit seafaring,
Hoisted the spruce tree to command a new world
Silent of bird voice.

None is so beautiful, whether undaunted
Flaunt I my colours close to wild wind's eye,
Or cleaving calm seas, gold on my spinnaker,
Dream down the evening.

Men say, who sight me naked on the pure sea,
Surely such craft once carried in his flame-spun
Pall a dead Viking past the horizon
Into Valhalla.

Land's End to Lewis I know, but I love best
My Western Islands where the rain purrs on
Blue profound anchorage, where the moon climbs
Over the Coolins.

When you are done with me, let me still be happy,
Wrap my ribs deep in the tides Hebridean;
And for a riding-light, clear above me,
Set the Aurora.

Cecil Day-Lewis

GEOLOGY

S KYE'S distinctive landscape is the product of millions of years of geologic change – igneous activity, deposition, deep-seated metamorphism, uplift and erosion by the action of ice, wind and rain, and the sea. The island is one of the most complex geological areas in Britain, and it is this complexity which is largely responsible for the island's varied topography.

To understand Skye's geological history, it is best to stop thinking of Skye as an island, as this was not the case until relatively recently. During much of geologic time the area which is now Skye was affected by the same geologic processes that shaped large areas of the northern Highland and the Hebrides.

The oldest rocks in north-west Scotland, and indeed Britain, date back over 2500 million years and were formed during a geological period termed the Pre-Cambrian. Lewisian gneiss, as this rock type is known, was formed from sedimentary and igneous rocks of much older landforms, which were buried and metamorphosed by heat and pressure over a period of millions of years. On Skye, Lewisian gneiss is exposed on the crags below Knock Castle in Sleat. It can also be found in outcrops throughout the Hebrides and the northern Highlands.

Nothing is known of the topography of the area during the early Pre-Cambrian, but by 1000 million years ago geologic evidence suggests that 'Skye' was on the eastern edge of a continent which stretched away to the north-west. To the south was a sea which covered much of the area now occupied by Britain, and to the north-west was a range of mountains, out of which numerous rivers flowed towards a flattened coastal plain, depositing thick beds of sediment in a sequence of sandstones and shales. These deposits now form the Torridonian sandstones of Sleat, which are several thousand metres thick in places.

By the Cambrian period, 590 million years ago, Strath, to the north of Sleat, was part of the eastern coast of a landform stretching to the north, south and west. Shallow seas advanced and retreated over the area, and sediment gradually built up to form conglomerates and sandstones, and in the deeper water, siltstones, shales and limestones. These rocks form a band crossing southern Skye and include the area around Allt nan Leac which has many underground caves caused by the erosion of the limestone, and the Skye marble deposits near Torrin. (The marble is limestone that was metamorphosed by a granite intrusion.)

Skye marble has been quarried at Torrin for many years. Slabs of this green and grey veined stone were used in the building of the high altar of Iona Abbey and the fireplace of Armadale Castle. Claims are also made that it was used in the decoration of the Vatican and the Palace of Versailles.

The Quirang

Geological evidence for the next 300 million years or so is missing on Skye, and the next rock formations encountered belong to the Triassic (240–200 million years old), the Jurassic (200–135 million years old) and the Cretaceous (135–65 million years old) periods.

Deposits from the Triassic – sandstones, marls and conglomerates – are mostly fluvial, formed from sediments on lake bottoms or on flood plains, whereas the Jurassic and Cretaceous sediments – limestones, shales and sandstones – were formed in marine environments, most of 'Skye' being under warm seas during these periods. Bands of these rock outcrops can be found at various points around the northern and western coast of Skye, most notably around the Trotternish peninsula. A further band crosses the top of the Strathaird peninsula. Rocks from these periods contain many fossils of plants and animals suited to warm and humid conditions, including corals, belemnites and ammonites. A fossil ichthyosaurus (fish-like marine reptile) of the Jurassic period was discovered near the shore at Rigg in 1966. It was headless, but still measured ten feet in length.

Much of Skye north of Strathaird has rocks belonging to the early part of the Tertiary period, dating to about 60 million years ago. By the early Tertiary period, the south and east of Britain had an outline roughly similar to the present day, but the north and west (although joined to the rest of 'Britain') were part of a large expanse of land which stretched as far as St Kilda to the west and southern Ireland to the south.

Skye was dominated by volcanic activity during the Tertiary period, and it is this which was responsible for the Black and Red Cuillin Hills, and the plateau basalts in

East side of the Quirang

Marsco

the north-west of the island. A volcano in the Kilchrist area erupted violently, shooting ash and lava over the land. Fissures opened, pouring out a steady stream of lava which built deposits up to 4,000 ft thick in north-west Skye, producing the rock masses which now form the Trotternish peninsula. Here the basaltic lavas almost completely buried the underlying Mesozoic rocks and it is only in the vertical cliff faces between Portree and Staffin that the earlier rocks can still be seen. These sedimentary rocks have been invaded by offshoots from a thick igneous sill, or sheet-like intrusion. This is best seen at the 'Kilt Rock', a high sea cliff which takes its name from the alternating light and dark banding of the igneous and sedimentary rocks.

Over a period of a few million years, the deep magma chamber which fed the volcanic activity on the Trotternish peninsula and the rest of Skye rose through the existing rock and cooled to form the gabbroic 'Black' Cuillins, the isolated Blaven Peak and the granitic Western and Eastern Red Hills.

Gradually this volcanic activity quietened and erosion began to slowly reshape the landscape. Some two million years ago extreme climatic changes occurred which would transform Skye and produce the features that we know today. Global temperatures, which had been gradually deteriorating, declined to a point at which continental glaciation resulted. Thick ice sheets spread over most of Britain north of the Bristol Channel. Glaciers moved west across the Highlands to the area which is now the Hebrides. As they moved, they scarred and scraped the rocks below. One such glacier flowed north, carving out the Sound of Raasay. Another gouged out a hollow which later filled with water and cut 'Skye' off from the Mainland. Lochs Snizort, Dunvegan and Slapin, among others, were formed at this time.

Smaller ice caps built up in mountainous areas such as the Cuillin Hills. Glaciers crept down the river valleys, cutting out massive U-shaped glens. The ice also carved out the deep corries for which the area is now famous. One of these corries, Loch Coruisk, has its bed 200 ft below sea level. It so impressed Sir Walter Scott on his visit to Skye, that his description of the area became one of the most dramatic passages in his poem *The Lord of the Isles* –

For rarely human eye has known
A scene so stern as that dread lake,
With its dark ledge of barren stone.
Seems that primeval earthquake's sway
Hath rent a strange and shatter'd way
Through the rude bosom of the hill,
And that each naked precipice,
Sable ravine, and dark abyss,
Tells of the outrage still.
The wildest glen, but this, can show
Some touch of Nature's genial glow;
On high Benmore green mosses grow,
And heath-bells bud in deep Glencroe,
And copse on Cruchan-Ben;
But here – above, around, below,
On mountain or in glen,
Nor tree, nor shrub, nor plant, nor flower,
Nor aught of vegetative power,
The weary eye may ken.
For all is rocks at random thrown,
Black waves, bare crags, and banks of stone,
As if were here denied
The summer sun, the spring's sweet dew,
That clothe with many a varied hue
The bleakest mountain-side.

The Quirang, West side

After the Ice Age, the sea level rose as the glaciers melted, though in some areas the land also rose as the weight of the ice was removed, forming raised beaches. These tend to be very fertile, and are found in Uig and Broadford among other areas.

Small freshwater lochs have since accumulated in the hollows formerly occupied by the ice sheets. Some of these were subsequently infilled with 'diatomite', the silicious skeletons of millions of tiny diatoms which lived in the lakes. Diatomite was quarried for industrial use in the early part of this century at several sites including Loch Cuithir. It has absorbent and filtering properties, and is also used in the manufacture of, among other things, toothpaste and silver polish.

Elsewhere the warming period at the end of the Ice Age led to instability in the massive basaltic strata deposited during the Tertiary period. As the ice sheets melted, the underlying clays and limestones could no longer support the basaltic mass, and the result was landslipping on a grand scale. The lava beds tilted forming a 'cuesta', with steep cliffs to the sea and gentler slopes inland. The poet and novelist Robert Buchanan, visiting Skye in 1883, wrote that the east coast of Trotternish had 'a panorama of cliff-scenery quite unmatched in Scotland', and described the cliffs as 'towering into the air like the fretwork of some Gothic temple, roofless to the sky'.

This line of precipices looms above the coast road between Portree and Staffin for almost twenty miles, the elevation seldom less than 1000 ft. Below the cliffs are pinnacles of lava which have slipped from the face, the most famous being the Old Man of Storr which is 160 ft high and can be found at the Portree end of the Trotternish Ridge. The Old Man is well-known among rock-climbers, although it was not conquered until 1955 when it was scaled by Don Whillan and James Barber.

At the north end of the Trotternish Ridge, above Staffin, is the Quirang, a jumble of peculiarly shaped pinnacles and rocks that have slipped from the cliff-face of Meall na Suiramach above. 'Quirang' means 'round fold', and it is said that four thousand cattle could have been concealed there in times of danger.

In contrast to the tipped landscape of Trotternish, the basaltic lava flows lie flat in the westernmost part of Duirinish. Each flow has a hard central portion, which is more resistant to weathering than the rock above and below. Because of this structure, weathering results in the formation of a stepped hillside, each step corresponding to a flow, the best example on Skye being the flat-topped 'MacLeod's Tables', Healaval Mhor and Healaval Bheag (Healaval Mhor is the shorter, but more bulky of the two).

MacLeod's Tables are said to have got their name from an escapade involving Alasdair Crotach, seventh Chief of the MacLeods of Dunvegan. In the early part of the sixteenth century he paid a visit to the King's palace in Edinburgh. There he met several lowland nobles who thought him too refined to fit in with their ideas of an island chief, and one of them challenged him, asking if Skye had such spacious halls, a larger table and more wonderful candelabra than those around them. The chief replied that he could certainly show him a more impressive roof, loftier table, and grander candelabra if the noble would make the journey to Skye.

The noble replied that he would make the trip just to prove him wrong. Great preparations were made at Dunvegan when word was received of the noble's arrival on Skye. It was late afternoon when the party arrived in Dunvegan, and they were taken immediately to Healaval Mhor. The sun was setting as they reached the flat summit which was covered with a huge banquet. All around stood MacLeod's clansmen bearing torches to light the scene. MacLeod commented that the roof was grander than any made by human hands, the clansmen more precious than any ornate candlesticks and his table larger than any in the royal court. The nobleman could only agree.

Erosion and the effects of freeze and thaw continue to sculpt the rocky mountainous landscape of Skye. The serrated appearance of the Black Cuillin Hills is due to the erosion of soft granitic dykes intruded into the gabbro. The Red Hills have fewer of these dykes and thus have a smoother conical outline. Their summits are covered in caps of frost-shattered detritus which has been likened to icing on a cake.

Soay from Sgurr na Stri

Kilt Rock, Trotternish

The sea also acts as a force of erosion. In some places where the rocks are less resistant to the rush of the tides, caves have been formed. Among these is Spar Cave at Glasnakille, visited by Sir Walter Scott in 1814, and recorded in his journal –

> The floor forms a deep and difficult ascent, and might be fancifully compared to a sheet of water, which, while it rushed whitening and foaming down a declivity, had been suddenly arrested and consolidated by the spell of an enchanter. Upon attaining the summit of this ascent, the cave descends with equal rapidity to the brink of a pool of the most limpid water about four or five yards broad. There opens beyond this pool a portal arch, with beautiful white chasing upon the sides, which promises a continuation of the cave . . . the pool on the brink of which we stood, surrounded by the most fanciful mouldings in a substance resembling white marble, and distinguished by the depth and purity of its waters, might be the bathing grotto of a Naiad.

Scott used his journal notes later in *The Lord of the Isles*. The cave of Glasnakille appears as the –

> . . . mermaid's alabaster grot
> Who bathes her limbs in sunless well
> Deep in Strathaird's enchanted cell.

Skye's geology is obviously responsible for variations in soil types and consequently the distribution of settlements throughout the island. The west of Sleat around Ord, for example, is very fertile and well-drained due to the underlying Cambrian limestones. The good crops which the soils produced, and the woodland which they supported, led to the area being known as the 'Garden of Skye'.

Peat covers vast areas of the island and its formation is the result of the wet climate and poor soil drainage. Rough grassland and heather cover much of the basalt plateau of northern and western Skye. Land over 400 ft is virtually uncultivated, although the upper areas of 'the hill' are often used for grazing. Within the Cuillin Hills there is very little vegetatation, with the summits being little more than naked rock. Skye's geology has largely determined the settlement pattern from the oldest known settlers to the inhabitants of today.

Blaaven

> O Blaaven, rocky Blaaven
> How I long to be with you again,
> To see lashed gulf and gully
> Smoke white in the windy rain –
> To see in the scarlet sunrise
> The mist–wreaths perish with heat,
> The wet rock slide with a trickling gleam˙
> Right down to the cataract's feet.

(from *Blaaven*, by Alexander Smith)

'The Castle', Quirang

ARCHAEOLOGY

JUST to the south of Skye, on the island of Rhum, archaeologists recently discovered traces of the earliest known settlement in Scotland, dating back 8500 years. A farmer's plough turned up a 'flint scatter', debris left from the manufacture of flint tools. The people who left the 'scatters' lived by hunting deer and small mammals, fishing the seas and lochs, and collecting wild fruits and nuts. Archaeologists call these hunter-gatherers 'Mesolithic'. Humans probably inhabited Scotland much earlier, but evidence of their existence may have been ground away by the actions of glaciers during the last Ice Age.

So far, no trace of Mesolithic habitation has been found on Skye, but as Rhum lies across a short stretch of sea, it is very probable that Skye's earliest settlements have yet to be discovered.

On Skye the earliest evidence of human occupation dates to the Neolithic period, around 3500 BC. The population were farmers, who grew barley and raised cows, sheep and pigs. Like the farmers of today, the early farming groups preferred the fertile soils of the coastal strip. The sea would have been important, both for fishing and for transportation.

The most obvious evidence of the Neolithic groups is their grand burial mounds, large cairns of stone with a chamber at the centre which housed successive generations of the dead. On Skye there are six chambered tombs, and four more possible sites. Rudh' an Dunain chambered cairn near Glen Brittle, excavated in the early 1930s by Sir Lindsay and Mrs Scott, is the best preserved.

The tomb is in an area remote from present settlements, but in the Neolithic period it would have been the focal point of a vibrant community, farming the fertile peninsula. Since excavation, the chamber has been left roofless, and the interior can be seen from above. The chamber walls were built with slabs of different kinds of igneous rock alternating with panels of drystone walling. In Neolithic times, the chamber could only have been reached by a low narrow passage which would have been blocked between burials.

The tomb at Rudh' an Dunain was used by two different groups of people. Fragments of the open-necked bowls of the Neolithic group which built the tomb were found in the chamber, along with bird, animal and human bones. The bones had not survived well, but some were identified as being from a middle-aged individual, probably male. In the upper part of the tomb were the remains of a later burial. Highly decorated 'beaker' pottery, dating to the early Bronze Age, had accompanied the remains of four adults.

At Rudh' an Dunain, as at many other chambered cairns, only a small fraction of the mound is taken up by the chamber itself, implying that the tombs were not purely functional. The massive heap of stones and earth enclosing the chamber was intended as an enduring testimony of the importance of the community whose dead were buried there. The large stone mound would have contrasted boldly with the bleakness of the surrounding landscape, and would have been visible from miles away.

Little is known of the spiritual beliefs of the Neolithic people, but it is probable that they revered the gods of the elements and the spirits of their ancestors. In a community which depended for its livelihood on favourable weather conditions for planting, sowing, harvesting and fishing, good weather was a blessing, and a spell of bad weather may have been seen as the anger of the gods. Everything possible would have been done to keep the gods' favour. Often bodies buried in chambered tombs were accompanied by pottery, personal objects such as a pin or dagger, and food

*anding stones,
re, Loch
izort Beag*

25

such as joints of meat, and grain. Such articles may have been placed with the dead to make their journey to the next world more comfortable, but it is equally possible that they were left there to appease the gods.

The houses and farms of the Neolithic communities are much more difficult to find, and in many cases, as on Skye, archaeologists have to rely on evidence from the tombs to build up a picture of the day-to-day life of these early farmers. As well as details on the animals kept and the crops grown, much information on the people themselves can be gleaned. For example, studies of human bones from tombs have shown that only about half the population reached twenty, and thirty would have been considered old.

More recent inhabitants of Skye treated the chambered tombs with a great deal of suspicion. When the chambered tomb at Liveras near Broadford pier was investigated in the 1830s, the first men to enter the chamber were armed with pistols to defend themselves from the strange animals thought to be waiting inside. In actuality all that was found were some charred skulls, several flint implements, pottery fragments and a stone wrist guard which would have been used to protect the hand while using a bow and arrow.

The great age of the chambered tombs was not always appreciated. According to folk tradition, the two massive cairns at Vatten in Duirinish were built on the site of the last great battle between the Clan MacLeod and the Clan Macdonald. A thick mist descended during the battle, causing great confusion, and resulting in the deaths of most of the warriors. So many were killed or wounded that there were no young men left to dig the graves, and all that could be done by the women, the old men and the children was to make two piles of the bodies, according to clan, and cover each with a heap of stones.

Another tale relates that one of the mounds at Vatten is the tomb of a powerful chief who owned most of the land in the area. He went on raiding expeditions each summer with his followers, bringing back gold, cattle, and slaves. One year his ships did not return when expected, and a few weeks later they were spotted sailing slowly into the bay. The chief had died on the expedition. His body was carried on the men's shields and buried in a grave piled high with stones to mark it. In the bay, his galley was ritually set alight and pushed out to sea. It is said that even these elaborate ceremonies did not placate the chief, and that his ghost still wanders the area.

In the nineteenth century a MacLeod chief began to excavate one of the tombs, but the work was heavy and the general feeling of the surrounding community was that the dead should not be meddled with. The workmen may have been afraid of encountering the 'barrow dweller', a strong ghost who forces to single combat those who disturb the grave.

Chambered tombs ceased to be built after about 2000 BC; the reason for this is unknown. By this time tools and weapons were being made from copper and bronze – the beginning of the Bronze Age in Scotland.

Bronze Age communities buried their dead in graves lined with stone slabs, sometimes covered with a small cairn of stones to mark the spot. Some of these cists, now empty, can be seen at Inver Aulavaig in Sleat. One was opened in the nineteenth century, and a skeleton in a crouched position was discovered inside. The bones were taken into the local schoolhouse which stood near the cairn but were only kept there for one night because of the loud 'whistlings' and other unusual noises which disrupted the sleep of the inhabitants.

Other reminders of the late Neolithic and Bronze Age in Skye are standing stones, such as the two stone sentinels at Eyre overlooking Loch Snizort Beag. The remains

Dun Beag, broch, Struan

of only three stone circles survive on the island, as well as two single stones, and one pair of stones. It is probable that many were uprooted during field clearance, or when Christianity spread to Skye.

A curious aspect of these monuments is that their location does not always coincide with a source of suitable stone. A block of stone would have been quarried and then transported, perhaps using rollers, to the chosen spot. Considerable effort would have been involved in moving the stone and in raising it to its upright position.

Few clues exist as to the purpose of the standing stones. Often they are loosely described as 'ritual' sites. Single stones may have marked out the edge of one tribe's territory; others seem to be associated with graves. A further theory is that the stones were astronomical alignments, used to time seasonal events such as the midsummer solstice.

In local legend, the standing stones are connected with the Féinn, a race of powerful giants – renowned hunters famous for their combat skills – believed to have originated in Ireland. It is related that the two stones at Eyre once had a third member, forming a tripod on which the Féinn placed an enormous pot large enough to stew deer whole (the Féinn had large appetites). Soon all the deer in the area had been hunted out and the giants had to look further afield for their food. One giant, Caoilte, was sent to the Cuillin Hills to hunt, but he was away for such a long time that the other giants got too hungry to wait. They collected whelks and limpets from the shore, and began to stew them. Suddenly there was a booming shout from the Cuillin Hills where Caoilte had located a herd of deer in a glen. At his shout, the giants tipped out their stew, which spattered the stones of the tripod as it fell. This is said to account for the mottled appearance of the standing stones.

The remains of Bronze Age settlements are, like those of the Neolithic, difficult to locate. 'Hut circles', the stone foundations of round huts, scatter the landscape, but these could belong to either the Neolithic, the Bronze, or the succeeding Iron Age. Earth-houses (thought to date to the later Iron Age) have also been found on Skye. They are long underground passages, which may have been cellar-like arrangements adjoining hut settlements above ground, the traces of which have largely disappeared.

Skye is perhaps best known among archaeologists for the remnants of its Iron Age defensive sites, the massively built brochs and duns.

Brochs were drystone towers, constructed with thick galleried walls, some reaching over forty feet in height. Two drystone walls were built side by side, and held together by horizontal stone slabs. (Single thickness walls of similar heights would have been very unstable.) Many of the Skye brochs were built on rocky knolls which would have made them look even higher.

Entrance to a broch was by way of a low narrow doorway which opened into a passage leading through the double walls to a central courtyard. Leading off the courtyard were entrances to cells, and also to a stairway which wound up between the walls to the upper storeys and the wallhead. Floors in the upper part of the broch were probably veranda-like structures, constructed of wood, with a central outlet for smoke. The dark interior would have been lit by oil lamps – stone or pottery dishes filled with animal fat or fish oil.

Brochs are found in the north and west of Scotland, and were built until about AD 100. Most of the twenty or so examples on Skye are in the northern part of the island.

Defence seems to have been a main consideration in the design of brochs. A heavy door could have been secured across the entrance passage, and barred from behind. Some brochs have guard cells at one or both sides of the passage, from which the bar could have been worked, once the identity of a visitor was established.

Anyone attacking a broch would have been faced with a high wall, blank apart from the well-protected door. A battering ram could have been used on the door, or fire brands lobbed over the wallheads to set fire to the wooden structures inside. But the broch defenders woud have had the advantage of height and a clear shot with arrows and stones.

Brochs would have been of limited use for a community whose animals were being pillaged, as it is unlikely that there would have been enough room inside to house sheep and cattle.

Evidence from excavations suggests that brochs were defended homesteads rather than refuges in times of danger. Dun Beag near Struan was excavated by Baroness Hanna von Etinghausen, the daughter of an Austrian baron. Her Skye connections were through her marriage to Norman MacLeod, twenty-fifth chief of the clan. He died in 1895, and the Baroness later married Count Vincent Baillet de Latour. The couple spent many of their summers on Skye, and between 1914 and 1920, the Countess, a keen antiquarian, directed excavations at Dun Beag.

Objects found during the excavations included bone and antler implements, stone whorls, a steatite cup (possibly a lamp) and some glass beads, and there were numerous decorated pottery shards, all suggesting permanent occupation.

Brochs serve a more sinister purpose in the folklore of the island. Tradition relates that the brochs were the dwellings of fairies, and the entrances to their country. Mortals and cattle carried off by the fairies were taken to the brochs, said to emanate an eerie green light when the sun went down.

A tale is related that one midsummer night at Dun Osdale, near Dunvegan, a man by the name of MacLeod was out on the moor trying to locate some cattle which had strayed. On reaching the broch he saw that the fairies were dancing around it, and he crept up to watch. Unfortunately a loud sneeze gave him away, and the fairies caught him and dragged him into the broch.

Inside, MacLeod was given a wooden cup ornamented with silver to drink from, but he knew that if he drank, he would be in the fairies' power forever, so he poured the wine inside his coat. The fairies, seeing the cup was empty, relaxed their guard and MacLeod escaped, taking the cup with him. The fairies pursued, but MacLeod reached home and his mother, who was a witch, put a protecting spell on him.

To counteract the witch's spell, the fairies cast a spell on the cup. Anyone who saw the cup would murder in order to possess it. The fairies soon had their revenge; MacLeod was murdered defending his cup. MacLeod's mother gave the cup – now free from enchantment – to the chief of the MacLeods, and it remained in Dunvegan Castle where it can still be seen today.

Many of the Skye brochs have the element 'dun' in their names, as in Dun Osdale and Dun Beag. This is a bit of a misnomer in strict archaeological terms, as 'dun' is used to describe a range of archaeological monuments distinct from brochs. Duns can range from small, thick-walled structures which could have been roofed, to large defended enclosures.

Most of Skye's duns are built in strongly defended locations, such as hilltops and the tips of promontories. Some of the largest duns are found on the Trotternish peninsula, one of the most fertile areas of Skye, and their size indicates that in prehistoric times this area supported a sizeable population.

Duns are usually built to incorporate the natural defences of a site. For example, at Dun Grugaig near Elgol, a high galleried wall was built across the neck of a coastal promontory, with sheer cliffs on all sides.

Dun Beag, broch, Struan

Like the brochs, duns were defensive structures. Some of the large duns were probably used for the coralling of livestock, while the smaller coastal duns may have been used as look-outs and signalling stations to warn the surrounding communities of impending danger.

What would the danger have been? Roman slave traders, or the tribes of mainland Scotland have been suggested. Alternatively, the problem could have been closer to home. In a society where wealth was measured by the size of a group's cattle and sheep stock, the threat of pilfering by neighbouring groups may have been a constant one.

> Upon a ruin by the desert shore,
> I sat one autumn day of utter peace,
> Watching a lustrous stream of vapour pour
> O'er Blaavin, fleece on fleece.
>
> The blue frith stretch'd in front without a sail,
> Huge boulders on the shore lay wreck'd and strown;
> Behind arose, storm-bleach'd and lichen-pale,
> Buttress and wall of stone.

(from *Dunskaith*, by Alexander Smith)

Pictish symbol stone, Tote

PICTS, VIKINGS AND EARLY CHRISTIANITY

S KYE'S history prior to medieval times is an incomplete tale, pieced together from a handful of written references, place-name evidence, and archaeology.

Much of what we know about Skye must be extrapolated from early Scottish history which is itself rather sketchy. Some of the earliest written references to Scotland speak of a people known as the Picts. The name 'Picti' means 'painted people' and was used by the Roman writer Eumenius to describe the population of northern Britain in the late third century AD. The use of the term 'Picti' did not imply a new group of people coming to Scotland; rather, it was the naming of the existing population.

The Pictish tribes occupied the area north of the Forth and Clyde, with the area corresponding to present-day Argyll being occupied by the Scots, incomers from Ireland, from about AD 500. The date at which a single Pictish kingdom developed is unclear, but it may have been as early as the mid-sixth century.

The only surviving written records attributable to the Picts is a list of their kings with the lengths of their reigns. Archaeologists also have problems with the period – it is difficult to find items which can be claimed as exclusively Pictish, although 'symbol stones' are one such item. About two hundred and fifty symbol stones survive in Scotland. Most are free-standing stones carved with between one and four motifs – mammals, snakes, and fish are included in the repertoire, as well as household objects such as mirrors and combs. Hundreds of motifs have been recorded, and many would have been understood throughout the Pictish lands. Some stones have crosses carved alongside the symbols; those without crosses are assumed to be earlier, belonging to the years before the north was Christianised.

Skye has three symbol stones (none of which has crosses), evidence that the Pictish lands included Skye. One of the stones was found lying on the beach at Fiscavaig and is now in the Royal Museum in Edinburgh. Another, found near the broch of Dun Osdale, is in Dunvegan Castle, and the third is in the open near Skeabost.

The purpose of the stones is unclear, but many theories exist. One interpretation is that symbol stones were set up near the sites of burials, perhaps recording the lineage and occupation of the deceased. Alternatively, the stones could be territorial boundary markers, denoting the groups which occupied an area. Dr Anthony Jackson, author of *The Symbol Stones of Scotland* has drawn attention to the fact that many of the symbols occur in pairs, and has suggested that the paired symbols tell of political alliances between groups, such as occasioned by the marriage of members of two tribes.

All three of the Skye stones have a crescent and V-rod symbol as part of their decoration. If we take Jackson's view, this might suggest that those who carved the stones all owed allegiance to one group.

Historical records tell nothing of the religion of the Picts before the beginning of Columba's mission. Iona was the religious centre of the Scots, and it was from here that St Columba set out to spread Christianity to the north of Scotland in the sixth century.

The spread of Christianity to Skye is not well documented. About a century after Columba's death, his *Life* was written by Adamnan, the ninth Abbot of Iona. According to Adamnan, Skye was the most northerly island that Columba visited, and two passages in the book refer to these visits. In one it is related that while in Skye, Columba came across a 'huge wild boar pursued by hounds', and slew the animal with words.

On another visit, Columba prophesied that during that day an old pagan man would arrive on the shore, and be baptised, die and be buried on the same spot. After an hour had passed, a boat arrived, and an old man, chief of the Genoa Cohort, was carried ashore, was instructed by the saint on Christianity, and the rest of the events followed as predicted.

Columba was patron saint of north Skye, while in the south, Maelrubha was revered. Until recently, the Festival of Maol Ruadh was celebrated on 25th August in Broadford. One of the places where Maelrubha is said to have preached is Ashaig, now the site of Skye's airstrip. Legend has it that he was looked on so kindly from above that good weather was always provided for him, and when he had no boat to make the journey to Skye from his base in Applecross, he merely sat on a flat stone and floated across the sea. At Ashaig, Maelrubha is reported to have kept his book of scriptures in a nook in a rock and worshipped from a crag. He hung a bell from a nearby ash tree which tolled by itself before each service.

Chapels or sites of chapels dedicated to Columba, Maelrubha and various other saints can be identified throughout the island. Many of the early Christian structures were built of wood and have long since decayed, leaving no trace apart from a name. The dedication of a chapel to a saint does not necessarily mean that the saint visited the site. Chapels dedicated to St Columba may in some cases just indicate an original connection with Iona. Later churches were often built on the sites of these early chapels. Bracadale Parish Church, for example, was built on the site of the ancient chapel of St Assind.

Monasteries were founded in Skye during the early Christian period. One such monastery was located beside Bay River on the Vaternish peninsula. 'Annait', as the site is known, means 'mother church', and this suggests that it is the location of the earliest Christian settlement in the area. The site lies on a neck of land between the river and a stream, and is an enclosure measuring about two hundred by one hundred and sixty feet. In the wall's thickness are the ruins of what were probably 'beehive cells', circular chambers used by monks as places of contemplation. Within the enclosure are the oblong foundations of what may have been a chapel. Bodies of unbaptised children were buried at the site until the end of last century.

Similar structures can be found on two 'islands', probably man-made, in Loch Chaluim Chille, in Kilmuir. The loch was drained in 1824. On one island are the remains of what were probably the living quarters of the religious community, and on the other island are the remains of a church. A causeway linked the two islets.

The extent to which Skye was Christianised is not known, and it is probable that the conversion was not always complete, but that the Christian god was added to the pantheon already worshipped. Some of the standing stones erected in Bronze Age times continued to be connected with ritual right up to the early Christian era. The presence of one or more standing stones near churches has often been noted. However, when incorporated into the Christian landscape, these stones were often 'Christianised'. The stone at Kilbride became 'Clach na h-Annait' – Stone of the Mother Church.

Another name for the stone at Kilbride is 'Clach na h-aindeoin', the Stone of Reluctance. The tradition is that an Orcadian pirate who took up Christianity made his crew promise that on his death he would be buried on Iona. When he died, the pirates set out for Iona, but were beaten back three times by a sudden storm. They took this as a sign that the pirate was too evil to be buried at such a holy site, and berthed at Strath burying their leader at the foot of the standing stone. The stone was named Clach na h-aindeoin, because the crew had unwillingly broken their vows.

A couple of centuries after Skye's conversion to Christianity, the Viking incursions began. The legacy of the Norse occupation of Skye and its effect on

Fladda-chùain from Lub Sco

Christianity is difficult to assess. Historians are hindered by a lack of written records, and many of the surviving accounts are biased, having been written by fearful Christians. According to Irish annalists, Skye was devastated from one end to the other during the first recorded attacks on the Hebrides in 794. Just as those on the receiving end of Viking violence may have exaggerated their suffering, it is probable that the Norse embellished their achievements in their accounts and sagas. However, it seems likely that Viking raiding missions continued to disrupt Skye and other parts of the North and West into the ninth century.

Not all Norse people came to the Hebrides to steal and destroy. During the 800s many were settling peacefully in the islands, refugees of problems in their homelands. They would have been converted to Christianity as they adapted their ways to those of the locals.

Scant physical evidence exists for the Norse presence on Skye. A grass-covered Bronze Age cairn on the foreshore of Tote, Skeabost, opened in the autumn of 1922, had a later Norse burial inserted into the top of the mound. A few fragments of charred bone and the end of a human femur were the only traces of a body. Objects associated with the burial included a heavy iron 'battle axe' weighing almost three pounds, and some fragments of iron attached to pieces of wood, which the excavator thought were the remains of a shield.

Legend has it that the old bourtree bush in the burial ground of St Congan's Chapel in Glendale grew from another Viking burial, from seeds in the pocket of the son of a Norwegian chief buried there. A crofter who cut some twigs from the tree and took them to his house had his sleep disrupted by the appearance of the Viking, protesting against the removal of the foliage. The crofter wisely returned the twigs to the burial gound next day.

Three hoards of Norse date have been found in Skye, but the findspot of only one is known. This hoard, containing one hundred and six Anglo Saxon and Oriental coins and twenty-three pieces of silver, including portions of bracelets and ingots, was found near the Old Man of Storr. From the dates of the coins it was probably deposited around AD 935.

Single Norse artifacts have occasionally been found, including a bronze buckle and a gold ring found during the excavations at Dun Beag and a penannular bronze brooch found in a bog near Bay. Although brochs like Dun Beag may have been re-inhabited by Norse people, the hoards and single finds are, unfortunately, of little help in determining the extent of Norse settlement on Skye.

No Norse longhouses have been found on Skye, although this may be due in part to the re-use of stones by later inhabitants. Remains of Norse settlements found in Orkney and Shetland suggest that longhouses on Skye would have been rectangular drystone buildings, about sixty-five feet in length, with rounded ends. A small walled area near the house would have been used for cultivation.

Perhaps the most effective method of determining the extent of Norse settlement on Skye is to plot placenames. Norse colonisation is thought to have begun in Orkney around AD 800, and spread to the northern Mainland, Shetland and the Western Isles from there. In Orkney and Shetland almost all the placenames are Norse in origin, suggesting extensive colonisation. Moving away from these centres, the density of Norse placenames thins out, indicating more patchy settlement.

Alan Small from Dundee University has tackled the problem of the relationship between placenames and Norse settlement on Skye. Although there are Norse 'landscape' names throughout Skye, Small has pointed out that this does not necessarily imply Norse settlement over the whole island. In plotting out areas of probable Norse habitation, he used only those names which suggest settlement, namely 'stadhr' (farm or dwelling place), 'setr' (dwelling) and 'bólstadhir' (farm).

Research by placename experts has shown that 'stadhr' is the earliest of this group of names, and it follows that places with the 'stadhr' element were among the earliest areas of settlement. In Skye placenames in this group end in 'sta', for example Connista and Shulista, and most are in the northern part of Trotternish. This pattern would be consistent with a population movement from the north, perhaps from Lewis and Harris. There are also a few 'stadhr' names around some of the larger bays on the north-west of the island.

The next oldest name in the sequence, 'setr', is represented in placenames by 'shader', for example, Uigshader. Again these names are concentrated in Trotternish, but there are additional groups around the south end of Loch Snizort, and the valley leading south-east to Portree. Small believes that this indicates the spreading out of settlement from those areas first occupied.

The final element in the sequence, 'bólstadhr' is represented by the 'bost' element, for example Colbost. Areas of settlement represented by this placename element lie around Loch Dunvegan, Loch Pooltiel, Loch Bracadale and Loch Slapin. From the 'stadhr', 'setr' and 'bost' names, the full extent of Norse settlement in Skye by the tenth century can be estimated.

Small believes that the settlement names and the more widespread landscape names indicate that the Norse eventually gained political control over the whole island, but that their main areas of settlement were in the north and west. He suggests that their occupation began with a short spell of warfare to establish supremacy, followed by peaceful co-existence with the natives.

Disagreement between the four kingdoms of mainland Scotland (Picts, Scots, Angles and Britons) is the most probable reason why the Norse were able to gain a foothold in Skye. The bickering meant that there was no united front to the Viking threat. In AD 843 when Kenneth MacAlpin, King of the Scots, and also a claimant to the Pictish throne, became 'King of all Land North of the Forth', the Norse hold in the Hebrides was as strong as ever.

The Gall-Gaedhil (Foreign Gaels), the amalgamation of native islanders and Norse settlers, are recorded as being 'restless and ungovernable' in the Norse sagas. The Scandinavian lands themselves became victims of raids from the Hebrides in the summer months. The *Ynglinga Saga* records that Harald of Norway, exasperated by these raids, 'went out with an army every summer, but when the Vikings perceived his army they always fled, and took refuge in the open sea. The king, becoming dissatisfied with these expeditions, followed the Vikings one summer with his army westwards over the sea. He fought many battles, in most of which he was victorious. He put to death the chiefs of the pirates, and he made indiscriminate slaughter of their followers'.

Harald's punishment of the Gall-Gaedhil was carried out in AD 888, but it seems that the lesson was soon forgotten, and shortly after Harald had returned home the raids began again. In 890 Kentil Flatneb was sent from Norway to sort out the rebels, but once there he took up the islanders' cause, 'and during his life he was master of the Hebrides'. His status was not accepted by Norway, and the struggle for control lasted for two centuries.

There are various occasions when the Gall-Gaedhil cooperated with the Scandinavians. In 1014, for example, according to an Irish account of the Battle of Clontarf, men from Skye fought for the Scandinavians against the Irish king, Brian Boru.

In 1097 Edgar, King of Scotland, formally ceded the Hebrides and Kintyre to Magnus Barelegs, who also established his authority over Orkney and the Isle of

Man. The treaty surrendered all those Western Isles where a 'helm-carrying ship' could pass between an island and the mainland.

During another period of unrest in 1102, Ingemund, a Norse viceroy in the Hebrides, was killed. This brought Magnus Barelegs' fleet from Norway to quell the rebels. In the *Magnus Saga* it is related that Skye was one of the restive islands –

Loch Coruisk

The peasant lost his lands and life
Who dared to bide the Norseman's strife.
The hungry battle-birds were filled
In Skye, with blood of foemen killed;
And wolves on Tiree's lonely shore
Died red their hairy jaws in gore.

After Magnus' death, Olaf the Red was chosen as leader of the islands. During his period of office, trouble broke out again on Skye, in 1140. Somerled, a chieftain of Argyll, but of Irish extraction, helped restore order. The *MS History of Clan Donald* relates that –

> Olay and Somerled killed MacLier, who possessed Strath in the Isle of Skye. They killed Godfrey Du by putting out his eyes, which was done by the hermit MacPoke, because Godfrey Du had killed his father formerly. Olay, surnamed the Red, killed MacNicoll in Uist likewise.

That same year Somerled married Olaf's daughter Ragnhildis.

By many battles Somerled succeeded in dividing the Norse Kingdom of Man and the Isles. He became leader of the islands south of Skye and Lewis, held from the Norse king, and of the area of Argyll, held from the King of Scotland.

Somerled's overconfidence led to his murder in 1164 while trying to conquer Scotland. After his death, Somerled's lands were divided among his three sons. Skye and Lewis remained part of the old Norse kingdom of Man and the Isles.

Throughout the thirteenth century, the Hebrides had increasing trouble with their mainland neighbours. The islands were frequently raided by the royalist armies, who, it is said, devastated villages and churches, and murdered children, picking them up on the end of their spears.

Alexander II of Scotland did not discourage the raids as he was determined to conquer the Western Isles and break their allegiance to the Kings of Norway. He died while carrying out his plan, but his young son, Alexander III, took up the cause and continued to encourage the Hebridean raids.

The Scots armies eventually invaded the Kingdom of Man. King Haakon of Norway appealed for assistance which came from Ruarie and Donald, grandsons of Somerled. The Scots army was defeated, but while Ruarie and Donald were gone, their lands were threatened and Ruarie appealed to King Haakon for help. On 15th July 1263, King Haakon sailed from Bergen with a fleet of one hundred and twenty ships and anchored at Kyleakin (Haco's Strait) on Skye where a great many other ships from all parts of the Hebrides joined the fleet. The Norwegian navy sailed south and was defeated by the Scots in August of the same year at the Battle of Largs.

Haakon died in Kirkwall on his way back to Norway, and the Hebrides, by the Treaty of Perth, signed by his successor Magnus in 1266, became part of Scotland. However, the islands remained largely unaffected by central authority, an independent territory under the Lordship of the Isles.

For Skye, this was not the end of the Viking story. It is related that some years after Largs an extensive raid was made on Trotternish. The Vikings were defeated and fled, all but one leader, Arco Bronmhor and some of his men who took refuge on the island in Loch Chaluim Chille.

A man named MacSween was commissioned by the Lord of the Isles to get rid of Arco, with the promise of the district of Braes as a reward if he succeeded. Brute force got him nowhere, so MacSween resorted to more subtle methods. Disguising himself as a bard, he was allowed to enter the island. After a song and a story Arco fell asleep and MacSween ensured that he never woke again. MacSween carried Arco's head in the folds of his plaid to his patron and was rewarded by being made tacksman of the Braes of Trotternish.

Dunvegan Castle

CLANS AND CASTLES

SKYE'S history from the thirteenth to the seventeenth century is largely the history of two powerful clans, the MacLeods and the Macdonalds, and their often bloody feuds for land and power.

The Gaelic 'clann' means merely kin, or family, and it is probable that clans like the MacLeods and Macdonalds rose out of the tribal organisation of ancient Celtic society which existed in the Highlands and Islands prior to medieval times. Kinship bound the members of these tribes together, and kinship was at the heart of clan society.

Before 1600 there were no 'clan lands' as such to which clansmen had rights of ownership; the bond between a clansman and his chief was all to do with kinship. Clan members did not always have a blood tie to the chief; the criterion for patronage was a willingness to conform to the regulations of the clan, the observance of the bond of manrent. Clan members had to serve their clan chief by land or sea as necessary, and also provide him with food. In return the chief defended and maintained the clan as he did his own family. The clan had two classes – 'saoi' (the warriors) and 'daoi' (the farmers and herders).

Although chiefship usually followed from father to son, an element of choice remained, and a chief's son could be passed over if he did not measure up to requirements. When this happened, however, the choice was still made from candidates from the 'reigning' line.

By medieval times the northern chiefs wielded a great deal of power. They acted as judges in matters of law; they decided when to make war and when to make peace. Even though Skye was part of a sheriffdom comprising Wester Ross, Glenelg, the Small Isles, and the Long Island, the powers of justice were still vested in the chief, who was allowed to retain a tenth of fines imposed.

Most of Skye, apart from Strath which was Mackinnon land, was occupied by the clan MacLeod by the thirteenth century. The origin of the clan is unclear. Leod is said to have been the son of Olaf the Black, and fosterson of Paul Balkeson, the Sheriff of Skye. With the help of Balkeson, Leod became lord of a large area of land including Uist and Harris (ceded to him on Balkeson's death), Lewis (from his father), Glenelg (from his grandfather) and Duirinish, Bracadale, Minginish, Lyndale and Trotternish on Skye (through his marriage to the daughter of a Norse potentate).

Norman, one of Leod's two sons, was the first chief of the MacLeods of Skye. He was an imposing figure, with a beard so long that he kept it tucked inside his belt. His Skye lands were held from the Earl of Ross, who had been given charge of the island by King Robert the Bruce. Norman's grave is on Iona.

Norman's son Malcolm (latterly known as 'the fat and good') succeeded him around 1320. Popular folklore connects Malcolm with the bull's head on the MacLeod Crest. The story goes that he was wandering alone in Glenelg one day when he was attacked by a wild bull. Malcolm fought with the bull so fiercely that he managed to pull one of its horns right off. The MacLeod motto 'Hold Fast' is said to have come from this encounter.

Skye's medieval history is largely tied up with the Lordship of the Isles, under which the west mainland and the western islands of Scotland existed as a political and cultural unit. Relations between the Lordship and the Crown varied with the Crown's strength. When the Crown was weak, the lords took full advantage of their position.

The title 'Ri Innse Gall', Lord of the Isles of the Strangers, was not a royal creation, but was adopted in 1336 by John of Islay, great great grandson of Somerled. Each successive Lord of the Isles and his Council assigned the lands of the Lordship as they saw fit. The service expected in return for the holding of lands varied. Army service (for the King's army) was sometimes required, but it was more usual for the provision of boats and crews to be specified. One charter, for example, stated that Malcolm MacLeod of Dunvegan was to hold part of Glenelg for a ship of twenty-six oars.

In 1335 Skye was conferred on John of Islay, first Lord of the Isles, by Edward Balliol, who had seized control of the Scottish Crown in 1332. But when David Bruce, the rightful king, was restored to the Scottish throne, he annulled the agreement and gave the control of Skye back to the Earl of Ross. John of Islay, however, later married the daughter of the Earl of Ross, and so again added Skye to the domain of the Lordship of the Isles.

Skye was to change hands again in 1382, when the island was granted to Alexander Stewart, Earl of Buchan, by King Robert II. This occurred during the chiefship of John, third chief of the MacLeods of Dunvegan.

John was known for his uncontrollable temper. While hunting in Harris he saw an albino stag which he wished to kill, but one of his retainers killed it before John had a chance. The huntsman was brought before John and disembowelled with the antlers of the dead stag. On the way back to Skye, the huntsman's friends attacked and killed MacLeod as he was boarding his galley. The boat, occupied only by his wife and daughters, drifted across the Minch, and was dashed to pieces on the rocks, now known as 'The Maidens', which lie below Idrigil Point. All on board were lost.

The fourth chief of the clan, the second son of John, was a churchman, William Cléireach, 'The Cleric'. Although trained for the church, William was a great warrior. In 1395, Donald, the son of the first Lord of the Isles, decided to take land from the MacLeods of Skye and confer it on one of his brothers. Donald's forces landed at Eynort in Minginish and made for the east, via Carbost and Drynort, leaving a trail of destruction. At the head of Loch Sligachan they met the resistance of an army of MacLeods. After the Battle of Sligachan it is recorded in the MacLeod Histories that the heads of the slain were collected and taken to Dunvegan Castle to be retained as trophies.

Much of the work which William Cléireach did to raise the standing of the clan was undone in the years following his death. William's son Iain Borb (the Truculent) was only ten when his father died, and a 'tutor' or regent was appointed to look after the clan affairs. The Macdonalds took advantage of the situation and again invaded the island, landing at Sleat and taking both Castle Camus and Dunscaith. They advanced to Dunvegan Castle but were met by the MacLeods of Skye and Lewis, a strong combined force. Iain was taken to Lewis by the chief of the MacLeods of Lewis who became his sponsor.

Dunscaith, now a ruin, occupied the whole summit of a precipitous rock overlooking Ob (bay) Gauscavaig, Loch Eishort. Thick walls surrounded the summit, and there was an oblong building within. The castle was cut off from the mainland by a trench twenty feet wide and sixteen feet deep, which had been hewn out of the rock. A wooden drawbridge would have spanned the gap. Dunscaith remained the principal seat of the Macdonalds on Skye until they moved to Duntulm.

Legend has it that Dunscaith Castle was built in a single night –

> All night the witch sang, and the castle grew
> Up from the rock, with tower and turrets crowned;
> All night she sang – when fell the morning dew
> 'Twas finished round and round . . .

Thus the Clan Macdonald obtained a permanent seat on Skye, heralding the beginning of decades of feuding between the MacLeods and Macdonalds over the right of ownership to various tracts of land.

The first chief of the Macdonalds of Sleat was Hugh, third son of Alexander, the third Lord of the Isles, and it is from him that the Macdonalds of Sleat derive their patronymic, 'Clann Uisdean'.

John, Hugh's brother, fourth Lord of the Isles, was forced by the king to forfeit his title in 1462, although it was restored on promise of good behaviour in 1476. However, this forfeiture had far-reaching consequences. Firstly, many of John's tenants were incensed at the submission. Secondly, they were irate that he had conferred lands on such tribes as the MacLeods and the MacLeans. John's son Angus Og, who was very ambitious, was backed by the chieftains to lead a revolt against his father. Civil war broke out. The MacLeods supported the old Lord of the Isles, while Donald, son of Hugh of Sleat, fought on the side of Angus Og.

The two sides met in 1480 in galleys off the coast of Ardnamurchan at a place known as Bloody Bay. Many of the MacLeods were killed, including William Dubh, the sixth chief. Later the Macdonalds of Sleat invaded the MacLeod territory in Skye to avenge them for taking the part of the Lord of the Isles. William's son Alasdair put up strong resistance, and routed the Macdonalds, but in the process was struck between the shoulder blades with an axe. His tendons were severed and he was deformed, becoming known as Alasdair Crotach (the Hunchback).

In 1482 Angus Og invaded Trotternish and took Duntulm Castle, then held by the MacLeods. Angus became Lord of Trotternish, and on his death the area was claimed by his uncle, Hugh of Sleat, Trotternish becoming yet another region of contention between the MacLeods and the Macdonalds.

John finally lost his title 'Lord of the Isles' in 1493, when it was abolished by King James IV. John became a monk in Paisley, and the chiefs now owed any lands in their possession to the King of Scotland. Although King James IV had abolished the Lordship of the Isles, he had not replaced it with any system that would allow the Crown to assert its own power, and the Highlands and Western Islands remained largely resistant to central control.

Feuding between the Skye clans over rights to certain areas raged. One of the fiercest assaults was carried out on the MacLeods of Skye by Do'ull Gruamach (Donald the Surly), fifth chief of Sleat, aided by the MacLeods of Lewis. They were aggrieved that the MacLeods of Dunvegan had been given a grant of land in North Uist and Sleat, and organised raids to expel the remaining MacLeods from Trotternish. Terrible atrocities were carried out as the inhabitants fled from the armies which had landed on the northern shores. The Skye MacLeods attempted to stop the progress of the army at Skeabost. The fleeing women and children were sent forward, and the men closed ranks behind them. Many of the soldiers were killed as they tried to cross Skeabost River, but the sheer size of the army soon sent the inhabitants fleeing again. As the heads of the slain flowed downstream they accumulated in a pool since known as 'Coire nan Ceann', the Cauldron of Heads. The Macdonalds eventually discontinued the pursuit and instead plundered the MacLeods' estates.

Alasdair Crotach complained to the Scottish government about the atrocities, and it was decreed that compensation should be paid. The scale of the devastation can be gauged from the compensation that was ordered, for example, Talisker had to be compensated for three hundred cows, one hundred horses, two thousand sheep, and an equal number of goats. There is no record of whether or not this was ever paid. The MacLeods returned to Trotternish some years later, but they were finally expelled by the forces of Donald Gorm, sixth chief of Sleat. The Macdonalds then moved their seat from Sleat to Duntulm Castle, which remained their headquarters until the eighteenth century.

Duntulm Castle is situated on a high promontory on the north side of Score Bay in Kilmuir. The promontory is only accessible from a narrow neck of land – it is inaccessible from the sea – and there are precipitous rocks on all other sides. The natural defences were enhanced by walls, trenches, and perhaps a moat. The MacLeods had spared no effort to make it an imposing castle.

In 1540 James V, gauging the seriousness of the situation in the Highlands, set sail for a tour of the north. He visited Duntulm Castle, and was very impressed by the natural strength of the site. The castle was abandoned around 1730, when the clan headquarters became the more modest Monkstadt House. In 1798, the principal residence of the Macdonalds again switched to Sleat, in Armadale, where the clan had a mansion. A larger house was constructed, known as Armadale Castle, although it was non-defensive.

The Macdonalds are said to have left Duntulm Castle for one of two reasons. The first is a family tragedy. One of the heirs is said to have fallen from the arms of his nurse and was dashed to death on the rocks below. Another tale is that the castle was haunted by the ghost of Donald Gorm Mor, eighth chief, who often returned with two ghostly companions to get drunk.

The main seat of the MacLeods of Skye was, as it has remained, Dunvegan Castle. The oldest part of the castle is the keep, a four storey tower used as a dwelling as well as for defensive purposes. Originally it was surrounded by a wall, making a courtyard, the only entrance being through the sea-gate. In the sixteenth century, Alasdair Crotach had another tower built – the 'fairy tower'. Later, in the seventeenth century a great hall was constructed in the space between the two towers. The entrance facade was erected early in the nineteenth century, and access was then made possible via a bridge. A further wing built later in the century, was the final addition.

Feuding was not always between clans; on occasions there were struggles for succession within a clan, as when William, eighth Chief of the MacLeods of

Dunvegan, died in 1551. The heir was only nine years old, and worse still, a female, Mary. The disagreement over wardship led to the Queen Regent, Mary of Guise, reserving it for herself.

The clan installed as chief Iain a' Chuil Bhàin, a great grandnephew of William Dubh, the sixth chief, skipping over Donald and Norman, the brothers of William, the eighth chief. Donald returned to Dunvegan towards the end of William's life, to stake his claims to the chiefship. The clan met at Lyndale to discuss the succession, and it was decided to leave Iain in possession, but that on his death the chiefship would revert to Donald or his heir, the original line.

That night Iain's second son, Iain Og, murdered Donald in his tent. He was expelled by the clan and turned to piracy under the protection of one Uisdean MacGhillespic Chléirich.

When Iain a' Chuil Bhàin died, the men of the clan raised his grandson, Norman, a minor, to the chiefship, naming as tutor a younger brother of Iain Og, Donald Breac.

While the clansmen were at Iain a' Chuil Bhàin's funeral, Iain Og entered Dunvegan Castle. On their return to the Castle, Norman and his brother Donald, and Donald Breac, the regent, were murdered as they emerged from the sea-gate. Iain Og assured the allegiance of the clansmen by holding as hostages the sons and daughters of the chief men of the clan.

When Mary had grown up, her guardian, the Duke of Argyll, decided that she should marry a Campbell, thus benefiting his clan, and he sent a contingent of the principal men of the Campbell clan to Skye to put forward this proposal. Iain Og invited them to Dunvegan, pretending to look on the mission favourably, and said he would abdicate in Mary's favour. The two parties banqueted at the castle, each of the Campbells sitting between two MacLeods. Later in the evening the attendants simultaneously placed a cup of blood in front of each of the Campbells. This was the pre-arranged signal for action, and every Campbell was killed.

By this time, Norman, the other brother of William, had entered into a bond of manrent with Argyll. When news of the massacre reached Argyll, Norman returned to Dunvegan to stake his claims to the chiefship. The most influential clansmen backed him. Iain escaped, leaving Norman as eleventh Chief of MacLeod.

Norman had many of Iain a' Chuil Bhàin's descendants murdered in order to strengthen his position. His relations with the clan became strained, and he feared for his own life. He formed a bodyguard of twelve men, each of whom had to demonstrate excellence in leaping, wrestling, throwing 'the stone', and tossing the caber, in order to join the group. The ultimate test was to wrench off a bull's leg at the knee with one hand.

Norman had a reputation for ruthlessness and is generally thought to be behind the infamous Massacre of Eigg. The incident was sparked off when some MacLeod youths, travelling from Mull to Dunvegan, stopped off at Eigg, a Macdonald territory, and while on the island insulted several local women. Offended Eigg men tied up the MacLeods, put them in their boat, and set it adrift. The wind took the boat to Dunvegan Loch, where the youths were picked up by their chief, returning home in his galley. Norman was outraged, and set sail with some of his clansmen for Eigg. When the Eigg people saw the galley approaching, they hid in a cave. MacLeod demanded that they leave the cave and surrender, but they refused. A large fire of turf and ferns was built at the mouth of the cave, and three hundred and ninety-five people are said to have suffocated.

But the Macdonalds soon got their revenge. One Sunday morning in the beginning of May, 1578, the Macdonalds of Uist sailed into the Bay of Ardmore in

Waternish. A large number of MacLeods were worshipping in Trumpan Church. The Macdonalds barred the door and set the thatched roof of the building on fire. Pleas for mercy from the terrified MacLeods were answered with 'You have taught us how to smother a people'.

One woman managed to escape and raised the alarm. A force of MacLeods arrived as the Macdonalds were rounding up the cattle of the district. The Macdonalds fled, but on reaching their boats found them beached by the low tide. In the resulting skirmish almost all the Macdonalds were killed, and their bodies laid along the bottom of a stone wall which was then pushed over to cover them. From then on the incident was known as the Battle of the Spoiling of the Dyke.

Brutal events such as these were not uncommon in the Highlands and Islands and led to various measures such as the passing of 'The General Band' by James VI, in 1587. The act forbade the chiefs to call their men to arms without royal approval. This did not put a stop to the feuding, however, and the chiefs were summoned to Edinburgh on the pretext of talks on better governing of the Highlands. But on their arrival the chiefs, including Donald Gorm Mor (the Macdonald chief) were imprisoned, and were not released until 1591, after paying heavy fines and providing hostages to ensure good behaviour. Later, in 1596, Donald Gorm Mor made his submission to the King and was pardoned. He was granted the heritable rights to the lands he occupied, except for parts of Uist and Trotternish. In return Castle Camus was to be maintained for the use of the King or his representatives whenever on visits to Skye.

A great deal of trouble in the late sixteenth century was caused by Uisdean MacGhillespic Chléirich. Uisdean was a renowned pirate and cattle thief. But sometime after 1596, he managed to convince Donald Gorm Mor that he was a reformed character. Donald, blinded to Uisdean's true motives, allowed him to build a castle at Cuidrach.

Castle Uisdean was of the peel type of fort, with seven-feet-thick walls, no windows on the ground level, and the only door eight feet above ground. When the castle was almost complete, Hugh wrote to his chief inviting him to a house-warming. On the same day he wrote a letter to a man named Martin whom he had hired to murder Donald Gorm Mor at the house-warming. The two letters became confused, and Donald Gorm Mor received the one detailing the plans for his own assassination. Hugh, realising what had happened, escaped to North Uist and hid in a fort called Dun na Sticir, but was captured and brought before the chief at Duntulm. He was thrown into the castle dungeons accompanied by a piece of salt beef and an empty pewter water pitcher. Uisdean realised his true fate on hearing the castle masons walling up the door to the vault. Years later when the dungeon was reopened, the skeleton was found clutching the chewed and twisted pitcher.

By the beginning of the seventeenth century the two main clans of Skye were again engaged in bitter feuding. This period is traditionally called 'Cogadh na Cailliche Caime', the 'War of the One-eyed Woman'. The trouble started after Margaret, a sister of Rory Mor (thirteenth Chief of the MacLeods of Dunvegan) was hand-fasted, or given in trial marriage, to Donald Gorm Mor. During the hand-fasting Margaret's eye became diseased, and she lost it. Donald Gorm Mor grew to detest Margaret as a result, and when the hand-fasting contract ended, he sent her back to Dunvegan on a one-eyed horse, escorted by a one-eyed groom, and followed by a one-eyed dog.

MacLeod was furious at this insult and demanded that Macdonald take Margaret back. Donald Gorm Mor refused, and the attacks and counter attacks began. The MacLeods attacked Macdonald lands in North Uist and Trotternish, and the Macdonalds attacked Harris, Minginish, and Bracadale. The culmination was a

Duntulm Castle

battle, in 1601, deep in the Cuillins at a place known thereafter as 'Coire na Creiche', or the Corry of the Foray. The Macdonalds, who had been raiding MacLeod lands, had driven several herds of stolen cattle to a rendezvous in the Cuillins, when they were set upon by the MacLeods of Lewis late in the afternoon. A pitched battle ensued most of the night and many were killed on each side before the Macdonalds emerged as victors. This was the last clan battle to be fought on Skye soil.

James VI was anxious to end the ceaseless feuding and ordered that MacLeod surrender to the Earl of Argyll and Macdonald to the Earl of Huntly, and that they should remain with these nobles until they had resolved their differences. A peace settlement was worked out, and to celebrate, a great festival was held at Dunvegan, Donald Gorm Mor and the principal cadets of the clan attending. The festivities went on for six days.

Over the next decade, various statutes and regulations were drawn up to curb the power of the chiefs. These included the loss of the chiefs' heritable jurisdiction, a recommendation that chiefs' children of over nine years old should be sent to the Lowlands to be educated, and a regulation which tried to restrict the consumption of wine. The chiefs were required to let out any land which they could not cultivate. Often this was done through a lease to a tacksman.

Rory Mor became a royal favourite, and was knighted by the King on a visit to London in 1613. James thought that this would induce better behaviour from the other chiefs, and his plan seems to have worked. In 1617 a subservient Donald Gorm (Donald Gorm Mor's son) was also knighted and raised to baronet in 1625.

Civil war broke out in England in 1642, but the Skye clans stayed out of the fighting at first. Sir Donald's son Sir James Mor eventually sent about four hundred men to fight on the side of Montrose, commander of the Royalist forces.

After the defeat of the Royalists on the field of Philiphaugh in 1649, a large part of the Highland army deserted. In 1650, Charles, son of the late king was crowned at Scone and received the support of the Scottish Covenanters. Many of the Macdonalds and MacLeods marched into England with the Covenanting Army, although the chiefs did not go. At Worcester, in September 1651, the Highlanders bore the full force of Cromwell's army. The MacLeods suffered most severely – about seven hundred out of a combined force of a thousand from Harris and Skye were slain. For several years after that the clan was exempted from military service to allow it to recover.

After the Restoration, Sir James won the favour of the Royalist Government, and began to frequent the southern cities, entertaining lavishly, and plunging the Macdonald estates into debt until his death in 1678. Similarly, Roderick 'The Witty', the fifteenth Chief of Dunvegan, spent most of his time from 1661 until his death in 1664 in the south, squandering his clan's fortunes.

A change had come over the clan chiefs which began to eat away at the long-standing trust that held the clans together. No longer interested in the culture of their own kin the chiefs began to exact higher rents to pay for their entertainment in the south. But despite all this the clansmen continued to revere their chiefs.

Highlanders were again called south during the 'Glorious Revolution' of 1688. The last Stuart King, James II, was deposed from the British throne and expelled from the country to put an end to absolute monarchy. James was considered too pro-Catholic for a Protestant country, and was replaced by his daughter Mary and her husband William of Orange. The Chief of the MacLeods of Dunvegan, Iain Breac, the sixteenth chief, busy trying to restore his estates after the excesses of his predecessor, kept his clansmen out of the fighting, depite the call of the house of Stuart. Sir Donald Macdonald, an ardent Loyalist like his father and grandfather, went with three hundred men when the Highland chiefs rose on behalf of King James.

Nothing would induce Sir Donald to recognise William as King, and he was ordered to forfeit his estates in June, 1690. Two frigates were sent to Skye, and an attack was made on Armadale where the mansion and a galley were set on fire, but the King's troops were routed. Donald later took advantage of an amnesty being extended to Highland chiefs who offered their allegiance to King William before the end of the year (1691).

Sir Donald was succeeded by his son, also Donald, the fourth Baronet, who, like his father, was a Jacobite supporting the Stuart cause. Donald sent men to fight for the Jacobite cause during Lord Mar's campaign of 1715 and 1716. When the government forces had regained control, the Macdonald lands were declared forfeit by the king, and remained forfeit until the chiefship of Sir Alexander. The commissioners of the forfeited estates advertised the lands for sale, before Sir Alexander was of age to be chief, but the principal clansmen bought the lands back for £21,000.

In the early eighteenth century, Norman, eighteenth Chief of the MacLeods, died. His son, also Norman, was born after his death, and the estates were held in trust. By the time that Norman succeeded to the lands, a great deal of money had accumulated due to the management skills of a small body of principal men. Norman however squandered much of this wealth, and even when the estate was heading for bankruptcy he continued to gamble.

Another of Norman's disgraces was his involvement in the abduction of Lady Grange. Her husband, Lord Grange, was a Jacobite; she was a Hanoverian. In 1730, Lord Grange held a meeting at his home in Edinburgh of some of those still committed to the Jacobite cause, those who favoured Prince Charles Edward Stuart, James II's eldest son, 'the King across the water'. Lady Grange found out about the meeting and threatened to disclose the activities of the group, which included Sir Alexander of Sleat and Norman MacLeod of Dunvegan.

Lord Grange and his friends decided that Lady Grange must not be allowed to betray them, and the decision was made to kidnap her and take her to the Highlands. As part of the plan, word was sent out next morning that she had died. Many people attended the funeral, where a coffin, filled with earth, was buried in Greyfriars Church, Edinburgh.

Lady Grange was taken to Idrigil, part of MacLeod's estate in Skye, but she managed to get word to her friends, and was moved to the island of Heisker, west of North Uist, when her captors again heard of a plot to rescue her. As her rescuers began to close in, Lady Grange was taken to St Kilda where she spent seven years. She was then moved back to Skye, and concealed in a cave near Idrigil Point. Once her faculties began to fail, and she was no longer considered a threat, Lady Grange was allowed to wander until she died in a cottar's hut in Waternish, and was buried beside Trumpan Church.

Sir Alexander and Norman MacLeod were also said to have been involved in the 'white slave trade', in the 'Soitheach nan Daoine' ('Ship of the People') affair. A huge demand for labour existed in the Americas during the eighteenth century, and high prices were paid for criminals and defeated soldiers, but those who ended up on a certain ship, *The William*, were neither.

In the spring of 1739, *The William*, said to be carrying brandy, sailed into Loch Bracadale. During the night, men from the ship went into houses in the area and forcibly removed inhabitants to the vessel, which then sailed to Harris for another round of kidnapping. *The William* arrived in Donaghadee in October 1739, with ninety-six people on board. As it had to be checked for the transatlantic voyage, those on board were taken to two barns until this could be done. Some managed to escape about two weeks later, and although recaptured, they aroused the suspicion of the authorities.

The ship's Irish captain, William Davidson, it was learned, was cooperating with a Norman MacLeod of Unish in Berneray, on the prospect of selling the islanders in America. Both MacLeod of Unish and William Davidson fled and were never brought to trial.

Many people felt that Sir Alexander Macdonald and Norman MacLeod of Dunvegan were at the bottom of the whole affair. As rumours abounded, Sir Alexander wrote to his lawyer Mackenzie of Dulvine, 'Last year MacLeod and I, in conversation we had, were regretting that we could not light on some effectual method for preventing theft on this isle . . . and we were agreed at last that the best method was to get some fellow that would take them on board a ship and carry them over to the Plantations . . .' In reality, none of those taken were criminals – sixty were women or children, and forty were men, none of whom had been convicted of any crime.

In 1745, the twenty-four year old Prince Charles Edward Stuart landed on the Island of Eriskay in the Outer Hebrides and began to rally support for his claim to the throne. Surprisingly, he did not receive any help from either Macdonald or

MacLeod. Considering Sir Alexander's loyalty to the Jacobite cause, and the loyalty of his predecessors, it is difficult to understand why he did not want to join the '45 rebellion. His wife, Lady Margaret, was also a Jacobite. One theory is that MacLeod and Macdonald wanted to keep out of trouble after the 'Soitheach nan Daoine' affair. They may have thought the risk of losing their lands too great, given the apparent hopelessness of the venture; Charles had only brought one ship of troops.

Given the odds, the Skye chiefs threw in their lot with the government, despite the fact that many of their clansmen were keen to fight for the Prince. Some of the clansmen even wore white cockades on leaving Skye, in the mistaken belief that they were going to fight for Prince Charles.

At Inverurie the Skye troops met a large number of Jacobites, and were pursued beyond the Spey. At this point many of the MacLeods deserted, but those who stayed marched on to Inverness where the government forces under the Earl of Loudon were holding the town. Loudon later attacked Moyhall, where the Prince had his headquarters. But Loudon's troops were tricked into thinking that an ambush had been laid, and retreated to Inverness.

The Prince's army marched on Inverness the following week, and as it approached, the government forces fled north. The remaining MacLeods made for Skye. Meanwhile, the Government had been assembling and training troops in Aberdeen. This well organised army met the Prince's smaller and less well equipped army on Culloden Moor near Inverness on 16th April. Hundreds of Highlanders died during the battle. On his defeat the Prince fled from the Government authorities, hiding in various places on the mainland, before making for Uist, helped by a Skyeman, Donald MacLeod.

Here he first became involved with Flora Macdonald. Flora was brought up on Skye. Her father died when she was a child, and her mother's second husband was a notable scion of the Macdonalds of Sleat. Flora was a favourite of Sir Alexander and Lady Margaret Macdonald, and often visited them at Monkstadt. They sent her to school in Edinburgh.

Flora was in Uist during the pursuit of the Prince, who by this time had a £30,000 price on his head. Flora's presence on the island was allegedly to visit her brother, but it is possible that Lady Margaret sent her to aid the Prince, and bring him back to Skye. The journey to Skye necessitated detailed planning as there were troops stationed all along the western shores of the island.

Flora's stepfather was a captain of troops stationed in Uist at the time of the Prince's escape. Had the captain not been kindly disposed to the Prince it is doubtful if the escape would have been possible. Flora obtained passports to Skye for herself, her escort, Neil MacEachain and 'Betty Burke', her maid (the Prince's alias). On 25th June the three boarded an open boat, the Prince dressed as Flora's maid, in a calico dress, a quilted petticoat, and a mantle and cap which covered his face. The five crew rowed all night, and the boat approached Waternish Point early next morning. Although they were fired on they managed to land safely in the afternoon at a point half a mile south-west of Monkstadt House. The Prince hid in a cave there.

Flora arrived at Monkstadt and informed Lady Margaret of the situation, avoiding the questions of some officers dining there. It was decided that Donald of Kingsburgh, a factor of Sir Alexander would take the Prince to Kingsburgh House where he was to spend the night.

From Kingsburgh House Donald and the Prince went to MacNab's Inn (now the Royal Hotel) in Portree, where they were joined by Flora who bade the Prince farewell. From Portree the Prince was taken to the island of Raasay and later to the south of Skye while plans were made to get him to the mainland where he could arrange transport to France.

Nine days after returning home to Sleat, Flora was arrested and taken to London where she was imprisoned until the Indemnity Act was passed in 1747. On her release she found herself instantly famous. A subscription was raised on her behalf to allow her to hire a post-chaise for Edinburgh. Three years later she married Allan Macdonald, eldest son of Macdonald of Kingsburgh. For twenty-two years they lived in Flodigarry, then moved to Kingsburgh House in 1772 on the death of Allan's father. Here they were visited by Boswell and Johnson.

High rents led them to emigrate to America in 1774. When the American War of Independence broke out, Allan joined the Royal Emigrant Regiment and was taken prisoner. Flora returned to Scotland and lived in Milton, South Uist until her husband returned to Skye. She died in 1790 and was buried in the churchyard of Kilmuir. A Celtic cross marks her grave, inscribed by Johnson's eulogy – 'A name that will be mentioned in history, and, if courage and fidelity be virtues, mentioned with honour'.

's ann 'na thigh mór
A fhuair mi am macnas,

Danns' le sunnd air
Urlar farsaing

An fhìdhleireachd 'gam
Chur a chadal

A' phìobaireachd
Mo dhùsgadh maidne

Thoir mo shoraidh, hó ó
Hóireann ó ho bhí o,
Gu Dùn Bheagain hì ó,
Ro Hóireann ó o hao o

In his great house
I have been joyful,

Dancing merry
on a wide floor

The fiddle-playing
to put me to sleep

The pipe-playing
to wake me in the morning

Bear my greeting
To Dunvegan

(from *Tuireadh* ('A Plaint'), by Mary MacLeod)

Folly built by Captain Fraser, Uig

CLEARANCE AND CHANGE

AFTER the defeat of the clans supporting Prince Charles at Culloden, the government took legislative steps to weaken and demoralise the Highlanders further. There was no distinction drawn between chiefs who had been loyal and those who had been disloyal to the government. In Skye, as in the rest of the Highlands, the wearing of the kilt, playing of bagpipes and carrying of arms were forbidden. At the same time, the speaking of Gaelic was discouraged.

Other less obvious changes were straining the very fabric of the clan system, namely the traditional relationship between the chief and his clansmen. These changes were slow, but steady. Some of the rebel leaders who had lost their lands were replaced by new landlords who did not hold the time-honoured values of Highland society. In addition, many chiefs were sending their sons to be educated in the South rather than using the long-standing system of fosterage.

Those heirs who came back brought very different ideas of how to run their estates. The others, preferring the lifestyle of the South, stayed there, leaving the management of their estates in the hands of factors. The mutual ties, trusts, responsibilities and loyalties which had held a clan together were being eroded and replaced by a relationship based much more on economics. The chiefs became landlords rather than the heart of the clan.

Boswell and Johnson, visiting Skye only twenty-eight years after Culloden, found that the clan system had already broken down. The system had previously depended to a large extent on a clansman's right to farm an area of land in return for armed service to the clan chief. Now that the Highlanders were no longer allowed to carry arms, the chiefs viewed the relationship differently. Johnson summed up the situation –

> The chiefs, divested of their prerogatives, necessarily turned their thoughts to the improvement of their revenues, and expect more rent, as they have less homage. The tenant, who is far from perceiving that his condition is made better in the same proportion, as that of his landlord is made worse, does not immediately see why his industry is to be taxed more heavily than before. He refuses to pay the demand, and is ejected; the ground is then let to a stranger, who perhaps brings a larger stock, but who, taking the land at its full price, treats with the laird upon equal terms, and considers him not as a chief, but as a trafficker in land. Thus the estate perhaps is improved, but the clan is broken.

In the Highlands during the second half of the eighteenth century, many chiefs grew rich through trading cattle with the South. In Skye about four thousand head of the small, sturdy, black cattle were driven to the southern markets each year. As demand for the cattle increased, so did the rents of the people occupying valuable grazing land. Further problems arose with the introduction of Cheviot and Blackface sheep farming into the Highlands. The price of wool was high, and lowland sheep farmers were keen to rent grazing tracts from northern landowners. In many cases the tenants lost not only the high moorland which they used for summer grazing, but also the land on which their houses stood. Expanding sheep operations drove them to more marginal land, much of it along the shoreline.

John Knox, a London bookseller who travelled through the Western Isles in the 1780s, understood the attraction of leasing land to sheep-graziers,

It need be no matter for surprise if a gentleman should embrace the tempting offers from sheep farmers. One man will occupy the land that starved fifty or more families; he gives a double or treble rent and is punctual to the day of payment.

Some of those who lost their land chose to emigrate. Word spread throughout the Highlands of new opportunities waiting across the ocean, the abundance of land. To people trying to eke out a living on small patches of infertile ground, the prospect was tempting. The reports sent back by the earliest emigrants encouraged many others to take advantage of the government-subsidised passages and join them. Between 1771 and 1790 about two thousand people set sail from Skye bound for America and Nova Scotia.

Boswell, visiting Armadale in 1773, found emigrants full of hope. Local people preparing to leave took part in a dance called 'America' to show their optimism. Anger and sorrow among those left behind soon gave way to a sense of resignation. Boswell related –

> Mrs McKinnon told me, that last year when a ship sailed from Portree for America, the people on shore were almost distracted when they saw their relations go off; they lay down on the ground, tumbled, and tore the grass with their teeth. This year there was not a tear shed. The people on shore seemed to think that they would soon follow.

Many of those who could not bear to leave their homeland were moved onto land subdivided from other crofts. Others were able to make their living in kelp production, and built houses along the seaside. The clan chiefs encouraged this latter option as, during the Napoleonic Wars, barilla (a marine plant used to make the alkali needed for glass and soap production) could not be imported. Kelp, made by the burning of seaweed, was a substitute for this. The prices were high, although the workers only got one tenth of the profits.

Given the financial returns, the Skye chiefs were keen to keep the kelp industry alive. Lord Macdonald was not pleased that many of his tenants were choosing to leave for America rather than settle on the small patches of land onto which they had been moved. Along with some of the other Highland landlords he negotiated legislation which pushed up the prices of transatlantic crossings beyond the means of the tenants. His kelp industry was thus secured, the proceeds helping to pay for the building of Armadale Castle in Sleat.

But in the 1820s the economic basis changed again. The import duty on barilla was lifted, and this, along with the beginnings of the production of Leblanc alkali in Glasgow, caused the prices paid for kelp to plummet from between £22 and £30 per ton to between £2 and £3 per ton. As well as being a disaster for the kelp workers, the collapse of the industry lost the clan chiefs a major source of income. Sheep farming was one of the few options left.

A population boom in the North made the situation worse. In 1755 an estimated 11,250 people lived on Skye. By 1841 that number had doubled. Several explanations have been put forward for this population boom: the relative lack of war and feuding, the introduction of the potato with its higher yield per acre and the discovery of the smallpox vaccination. Pressure on already overcrowded marginal land became even greater and the better land was divided and subdivided among families until it was overworked to the point of infertility.

Massive clearance was the inevitable consequence. Up to two thousand people were dispossessed from the MacLeod estates alone. In 1826 and 1827 at least thirteen

Glendale

hundred people left Skye for America and Canada. Some had received eviction notices and applied for government-assisted passages. Others had no option. In 1830, for example, the following statement was read by the sheriff officer to the ten families living in Lorgill, an isolated glen near Glendale –

To all the crofters in Lorgill. Take notice that you are hereby duly warned that you all be ready to leave Lorgill at twelve o'clock on the 4th August next with all your baggage but no stock and proceed to Loch Snizort, where you will board the ship *Midlothian* (Captain Morrison) that will take you to Nova-Scotia, where you are to receive a free grant of land from Her Majesty's Government. Take further notice that any crofter disobeying this order will be immediately arrested and taken to prison. All persons over seventy years of age and who have no relatives to look after them will be taken care of in the County Poorhouse. This order is final and no appeal to the Government will be considered. God Save the Queen.

There is no road to Lorgill, just the track from Ramasaig, the next glen. On reaching the village you can look down the valley to the sea at the bottom. Along each side of the river are the grass-covered ruins of the stone-built cottages. It is easy to imagine the life of the small community which once inhabited it, and the final sad trek to Loch Snizort.

Lorgill was not the only village left empty; many other straths were cleared. Families were evicted from Duirinish, Bracadale and Minginish. In forty years, from 1841 to 1881, the population of 1824 was halved. Tenant farmers replaced the crofters, six of them in this area, at Talisker, Glenbrittle, Drynoch, Ebost, Ose and Totarder.

Between 1851 and 1853 Lord Macdonald's factor cleared the villages of Boreraig and Suisinish. The reason given to the crofters was over-population. Ten families received summons and were shipped off in the *Hercules*. A deadly fever broke out and many on board that ship got no further than Cork. Those who had been permitted to remain in Skye were all ordered to leave their houses on 4th April 1853. They were informed that land would be found for them elsewhere on the estate, but the land they were offered was unsuitable for cultivation and many families refused to leave their homes.

In mid-September, Lord Macdonald's officer and a number of constables arrived in the glens, and proceeded with the evictions of the remaining thirty-two families. The action was taken at a time when most of the men were working away from home. Furniture was thrown from the houses, the aged and infirm taken outside, and the cottages padlocked.

An eye-witness, Donald Ross, told how Flora Robertson, a ninety-six year old grandmother was evicted. She was living with her son, a widower, who was away from home, and his four children. The children had lifted their grandmother from her bed and taken her outside to sit in the fresh air. Shortly after this the children heard dogs barking and set off to investigate. Furniture was being thrown out of their neighbours' cottage. Returning to their own cottage they tried to take their grandmother back inside, but they were too late. The officers appeared and threw out the furniture, barring and padlocking the door. The old lady could not travel, and anyway, the family had nowhere to go. The children managed to get the old woman to a sheep-cot where they remained until December, when their father returned, but he became ill and died in the damp and cold of the sheep-cot. Eventually the children and their grandmother were moved to a house in another area by the inspector of the poor (an officer of Lord Macdonald).

Ullinish and Loch Bracadale

In the case of Boreraig and Suisinish, it is hard to believe that the clearances were intended to ease over-population. If this had been the aim, only a few families, rather than whole villages, would have been moved.

The late nineteenth century Skye poet Neil MacLeod captures his feeling of sadness at the deserted villages in his poem *An Gleann 's an robh mi òg* (The Glen where I was Young) –

Tha na fàrdaichean 'n am fàsach	The dwellings are desolate
Far an d'araicheadh na seòid,	Where warriors were reared,
Far'm bu chridheil fuaim n gàire	Where hearty was the sound of their laughter,
Far'm bu chàirdeil iad mu'n bhòrd	Where they were hospitable round the table,
Far am faigheadh coigreach bàigh	Where the alien would find kindness
Agus ànrach bochd a lòn	And the poor stranger, food,
Ach chàn fhaigh iad sin 'san àm so	But they will not get that at this time,
Anns a' ghleann 's an robh mi òg.	In the glen where I was young.

The poverty of the nineteenth-century Skye people cannot be blamed totally on the landlords. Bad harvests in 1835 and 1836 were followed by the total failure of the potato crop in 1846 and 1847. Money raised in the South as relief for famine victims was topped up by the chiefs. Various government subsidised work schemes were tried out, such as the food depot established in Portree in 1846. Eight hours of work earned a labourer one and a half pounds of meal, plus half a pound for every child in the family and three quarters of a pound for his wife.

Despite these attempts to ease the hardship, there was no getting away from it – in the eyes of many landlords the crofters were a burden rather than a source of income. Sheep farmers were a more viable alternative.

Yet even if the economic situation was impossible, it is the lack of concern for the people themselves – the idea that they had no right to decide their own destiny – which seems so harsh. Landlords often fell back on the excuse that they were evicting the crofters 'for their own good'.

Many of the ships used to transport the dispossessed were overcrowded and unsuitable for passengers. In 1834 alone more than seven hundred emigrants died in Atlantic shipwrecks. It could take as long as ten to fifteen weeks to reach the other side, and smallpox, typhus and diphtheria spread quickly in the cramped and unsanitary conditions. In some ways the conditions were worse than on slaving ships – the value of slaves depended on their condition when they reached their destination. The Highland people had already paid for their passages on boarding, thus the ship-owners had no incentive to worry about conditions on board.

For people to have boarded these unhappy ships with little or no resistance may seem surprising, but less so when the combined front of landlords and the Church is considered. In the minds of most people, clan loyalty was still important, and a chief's orders were to be obeyed. The Church often backed the ambitions of the chiefs, persuading congregations that the evictions were God's will. In some areas the ministers were offered an acre of land by the landlord for every family that they persuaded to emigrate. In 1843 when the Free Church broke away from the Church of Scotland, the crofters at last found a powerful ally.

The crofters' cause was eventually brought to the attention of the British public by newspaper reports. Northern newspapers such as *The Highlander* were first to print articles on the Clearances in Skye and other areas, but the issue soon became one of national interest.

Overleaf: Late evening, from Sconser Lodge

One event which attracted the attention of the press occurred on 13th October 1877. A freak rainstorm dropped an estimated seven inches of rain on the hills above Uig that day. Two rivers burst their banks, joined forces, and brought boulders, vegetation and mud crashing down towards the Bay. Bridges were torn away in the torrent which then swept through Uig cemetery before ploughing into Uig Lodge, the home of Captain Fraser, a landlord noted for his relentless way with crofters. Captain Fraser was not at home at the time, but his estate manager was killed in the flood. When the waters receded, the gardens of the Lodge were littered with bones from the cemetery.

The Highlander had this to say about the catastrophe –

> The belief is common throughout the parish that the disaster is a judgement upon Captain Fraser's property. It is very remarkable, it is said, that all the destruction on Skye should be on his estate. What looks so singular is that two rivers should break through every barrier and aim at Captain Fraser's house. Again, it is strange that nearly all the dead buried in Uig in the last five hundred years should be brought up as it were against his house, as if the dead in their graves rose to perform the work of vengeance which the living had not the spirit to execute. But although the living would not put forth a hand against the laird, they do not hesitate to express their regret that the proprietor was not in the place of the manager when he was swept away. It is sadder than the destruction itself that such feeling should be kindled under the land laws of Great Britain.

Captain Fraser responded to this insult by suing the editor of the newspaper, John Murdoch, for £1000, but was awarded only £50 plus costs. If Fraser's aim had been to intimidate the press, it did not work. Neither he nor the other landlords of the North had seen the last of the attentions of the press.

As clearances continued over the next few years, the frustrations of the crofters built up to boiling point. A significant day in crofting history was 21st February 1882. John MacPherson of Glendale held a public meeting to set up a Land League. Not only was the subject matter risky, so too was the actual holding of the meeting. Any gathering of more than three people not in the same family had been prohibited by the landlord with the support of the Sheriff. Eviction and shipping were the penalties which the crofters risked. Potential disaster was averted by the local Free Church minister, Revd MacRae, who allowed the meeting to be held on church ground.

In his address MacPherson challenged the evictions, pointing out that a fundamental principle of the clan system was that the land belonged to the clan, and was not the personal property of the clan chief. The people of Glendale decided to put their animals onto Waterstein estate in defiance of an interdict of the Court of Session. An officer of the Court was sent to Glendale with writs, but these were refused by the crofters.

The county officials applied for government help which was sent in the form of a gunboat, the *Jackal*. It anchored in Loch Pooltiel, the bay at Glendale. An officer and a group of marines came into the glen to arrest MacPherson and his leading supporters. MacPherson and two others surrendered and were taken south to appear in court in Edinburgh, but on reaching Glasgow they were forcibly arrested in their hotel.

The 'Incorrigible Rogues of Glendale', as they were called by some newspapers, each had to serve two months in prison. Throughout the Highlands and Islands the defiance of the 'Glendale Martyr' spurred crofters on to similar acts. On his release,

MacPherson spoke throughout the North, encouraging more people to join the Land League, also known as the Highland Land Reform Association.

Resistance was put up in other parts of Skye too, including Macdonald's land at Braes near Portree, and Captain Fraser's estates at Kilmuir.

As at Glendale, grazing rights were at the heart of the troubles at Braes. The Braes crofters wanted to graze their sheep on nearby Ben Lee, a right which had been taken from them in 1865. The grazier's lease had expired, and the Braes crofters offered to pay a higher price to secure their right to the grazing. Their offer was refused, so some of the crofters withheld their rent.

This brought the Sheriff's officer (also Lord Macdonald's deputy factor) with eviction notices. He was met by the Braes community which forced him to burn the summonses on the public highway.

Fifty constables from Glasgow were sent to put down the Braes rebels. Led by Sheriff Ivory of Inverness-shire, they made a dawn raid on Braes on 19th April 1882, to arrest the five ringleaders. The earliness of the hour surprised the villagers, but by the time the arrests had been made and the police were once more heading for Portree with their prisoners, the men, women and children of Braes had gathered at Gedintailor. Here the road narrows with a steep slope to the sea on one side, and the mountainside on the other. An ambush was set, and as the entourage reached the spot, the crofters began to pelt the constables with rocks and stones. Batons were drawn and the police charged the crowd and won through. Many people were hurt in the raid, including Sheriff Ivory. The offenders were tried in Inverness and fined, but this did not deter the people of Braes from continuing to graze their sheep on Ben Lee.

The plight of the Braes crofters won sympathy through the national press, and the dilemma of the Highland crofters in general soon became a matter of political concern, one of urgent importance on the parliamentary agenda.

A major outcome of this interest in the North was the setting up of a Royal Commission made up of three landowners – Francis Napier, Baron of Napier and Ettrick who was head of the Commission; Donald Cameron of Lochiel and Sir Kenneth MacKenzie of Gairloch, also, Donald MacKinnon, a professor of Celtic; Charles Fraser MacIntosh, Liberal MP for the Inverness burghs and a campaigner for crofters' rights; and Alexander Nicholson (a Skye man), Sheriff Substitute at Kirkcudbright.

The Royal Commission arrived at Braes Church in May 1883 and heard the first of almost eight hundred statements recorded during a tour of the Highlands and Islands which took over five months. John MacPherson, the 'Glendale Martyr', was among those whose evidence was heard.

Crofters throughout the North were gaining confidence, and showing it by grazing their cattle on restricted areas. On Skye especially, the situation was getting out of control. Revolvers and ammunition were sent to the Skye police by the Home Office, followed by six additional policemen.

In areas such as Captain Fraser's Kilmuir, it was virtually 'no go' for the police. Some of the tenants in this area were on rent strike, and Fraser decided to evict forty of them, including all the local members of the Land League. The Sheriff's Officer who came to serve the writs was attacked and chased off.

Eventually the decision was made to send in troops. Four ships – the *Lochiel, Banterer, Forester* and *Assistance* arrived with about five hundred marines and fifty armed police. The convoy sailed into Uig Bay, and Sheriff Ivory, now recovered from the Battle of Braes, led two hundred and fifty of the troops to Kilmuir.

The people of Kilmuir told the press that their disagreement was with the landlord, not the military, and they had hoisted a Union Jack from one of the crofts to stress

Coral Beach, near Dunvegan

this point. The whole effect was one of overkill, and from London the Home Secretary sent a message to Ivory stating his surprise at the use of so many heavily armed men to evict unarmed crofters.

Similar peaceful demonstrations greeted the forces at Glendale where the crofters had agreed not to remove their stock and to resist arrest, but to do it peacefully. The forces stormed Glendale and dispersed a meeting of six hundred Land Leaguers on Colbost Hill. They then garrisoned themselves in Hamera Lodge in an attempt to intimidate the crofters, all to no avail.

The Napier Commission announced its recommendations in 1884. These did not go far enough for either landlord or tenant. Only the crofters with most land were to have security of tenure – the rest would still be exposed to eviction. Secondly, it was suggested that the Highland township was to be run as a commune with joint-owned arable and pasture. If the amount of land available to a township was insufficient, adjacent land could be compulsorily purchased.

The main aim of the Land Leaguers had been to secure tenure for every crofter, and of course the landowners were not impressed.

Prime Minister Gladstone ignored the recommendations and passed the Crofters' Holdings Act in 1886, which was similar to his 1881 Land Act for Ireland. An independent body was to fix rents, and on paying these 'fair' rents, the crofters earned security of tenure. Tenants could also leave their crofts by inheritance. However, the Act did not go far to reallocate land to crofters who had already lost it through clearance.

Security of tenure was a great victory for the crofters. The Kilmuir Estate, for example, was bought by the Congested Districts Board and its sheep farms divided into crofts.

John MacPherson continued his campaign for ownership. In Glendale the lands of the estate were purchased by the Congested District Commission and sold to the crofters. Each crofter received a share in the estate and a share in the common grazing. MacPherson had realised his aim. Even today the Estate is run by the people of Glendale through a committee of management elected by the shareholders.

The crofters' fight had been long and hard, but their gains must have exceeded even their wildest hopes. However, many crofters did not take the chance of buying their land as had been done in Glendale, and so the ultimate aims of John MacPherson were not realised outwith his own community.

RELIGION

THE Columban-Celtic Church, founded in the sixth century, served the Highlands and Islands for over five hundred years. Despite the Church's longevity, various problems kept it from wielding the influence it might have had over the scattered communities of the North and West. No real bonds existed between the heads of different monasteries, for example. And the scriptures were in Latin, with little scope for translation into English, far less Gaelic.

By the twelfth century, Norse influence in the Western Isles had extended to religious matters. In 1154 the diocese of the Isles was put under Norwegian control, although the patronage of the see, based on the Isle of Man, was transferred to the King of Scots in 1266. The location of the Cathedral of the Isles from the latter part of the thirteenth century is not known with certainty, although it seems to have been at Snizort in Skye by 1433, from where Bishop Angus of the Isles petitioned the Pope to allow him to move to 'some honest place within the diocese'.

In 1506, the Abbey of Iona became the seat of the Scottish diocese of the Isles, and by 1561 the Abbot held rights to land in certain areas of Skye, including Armadale, and claimed churches such as Kilmore in Sleat and the church at Snizort.

Of the churches under lay patronage, one third of the teinds went to the bishop. Free hospitality offered in 'God's name', was a constant drain on the resources of the churches. Maintenance of the church buildings was another major expense, as many were in constant disrepair. Papal indulgences were granted in 1382 to those who visited the chapel of St Columba in Duirinish and contributed to its repair.

During the early years of the sixteenth century, James IV set out to reform his Highland subjects through the influence of the Church. He made a large number of presentations to churches in Skye, among other areas. Protection had to be given to the rectors in the lawless conditions that prevailed. In 1507, the rector of Kilmuir in Trotternish was granted a letter of protection from the king against those who might attempt to steal the church's property.

Little is known of religious life in Skye in the early sixteenth century – it would appear that for years no great regard was paid to the needs of the church. One of the ecclesiastical buildings in Skye thought to date to the years before the Reformation is the ruined church of Kilchrist between Broadford and Torrin, a simple rectangular building which measured just over fifty by seventeen feet internally. The ground between the church and the loch at Kilchrist is still known as the Hill of the Mass.

The Reformation came to Scotland later than England. In 1517, Martin Luther nailed his Theses to the church door at Wittenberg, and early in the 1530s, Henry VIII took up the Protestant cause. Gradually, although banned by the Scottish Parliament, English translations of the Bible began to appear in Scotland. Discontent with the Church was growing, and a popular movement for reform was spreading.

In 1557 the document which became known as the First Covenant was drawn up, and those who signed pledged that they would break with Rome and set up a reformed church. Their demands included Communion in both kinds and the holding of religious services in English rather than Latin. Both Parliament and the clergy turned down their requests.

It was not until 1560, after the death of Mary Queen of Scots' mother, Marie de Guise, a powerful campaigner for the retention of Catholicism, that Parliamentary Acts were draw up for the final break with Rome.

The early Scottish Kirk was austere in character. Christmas and Easter were no longer observed, churches were undecorated and there was no musical accompaniment to the singing. Whereas in England the Reformed Church was still governed by a hierarchy of bishops and archbishops, the new Scottish Church was governed by a kirk session of lay elders and later by district Presbyteries. A General Assembly of ministers and laymen met every year to discuss questions affecting the Kirk as a whole.

The General Assembly of 1560 appointed five superintendents to oversee the appointment of ministers and the establishment of kirks throughout Scotland. This was a difficult task due to the lack of ministers qualified in the new faith. No church records exist for the district of Argyll and the Isles before 1638, and there is only mention of two Protestant ministers being placed in the district, one of those being Malcolm MacPherson, who was presented to the parish of Duirinish in 1566.

The extent to which the Highlands and Islands cast off Roman Catholicism at this point cannot be accurately assessed. But the principal clan chiefs probably had no scruples about getting rid of their ties with the Catholic Church, if it would further their ambitions, and it is to be assumed that the clan members followed their chiefs in religious as well as secular matters. Donald Gormson, seventh chief of the Macdonalds of Sleat, received favours for his 'faithful service' to the government, which might indicate that he had taken up the Protestant cause. He died in 1573, and the Reformation must have reached Skye through him by then.

The regent, James Gruamach, who looked after the Macdonald affairs during the minority of Donald Gormson's son, Donald Gorm Mor, was not as zealous in upholding the Protestant cause. In 1575 the government made him sign a bond whereby he promised to pay to the Bishop of the Isles the teinds due for the lands of Sleat and Trotternish. Similar citations were served on other landowners of Skye.

In this transitionary period then, it seems that the Church and its affairs were neglected on Skye. Churches fell into disrepair, and stipends were not paid regularly to the incumbents. The preface to the *Statutes of Iona* comments on the state of the Church in the Isles at the beginning of the seventeenth century, stressing the 'great ignorance' of the chiefs and the people, stemming from both the lack of ministers and the contempt for those already there. Under pressure from the Crown, a bond was signed in 1609 by the Skye chiefs, Donald Gorm Mor, Rory Mor and Lachlan MacKinnon declaring that they would support the 'true religion'.

Although James VI supported the Protestant cause, he believed that the church should be governed, as in England, by bishops appointed by the Crown. James ignored the wishes of the Kirk and statutes were passed endorsing the appointment of bishops, but he eventually had to give in due to the outrage which this caused.

James's successor, Charles I, again demanded that religious practice in Scotland should conform to that of England. Among other measures, a prayer book was drawn up for Scotland to take the place of 'impromptu' prayer. In response, hundreds of nobles and gentry signed a document which became known as the National Covenant. At the General Assembly of 1638, the Prayer Book was abolished and all the bishops were deposed.

In 1643, during the Civil War, the English Parliament, facing defeat from the Royalist forces, turned to the Scottish Covenanters for support. A document known as the Solemn League and Covenant was agreed, under which the Covenanters undertook to attack the Royalist forces from the North in return for a total reform of religious practices in England and Ireland, a rooting out of all vestiges of papistry. A body of clergy and laymen including eight Scottish delegates, known as the Westminster Assembly, met to establish a unified form of worship. The outcome was the Westminster Confession of Faith, which although having little effect on

Church, Kensaleyre

England and Ireland, forms the basis of Presbyterian religion in Scotland. At this time there were also concerted efforts to secure a Gaelic-speaking ministry for the Highlands.

Certain features of the present-day Presbyterian Church stem from this period. By the early seventeenth century the custom of 'lining out' was established – a precentor chanted each line of a psalm which was repeated by the congregation, and so on to the end. The congregation sat to sing, and stood to pray. Because so few Highlanders could read Gaelic, 'lining out' became an established tradition.

During the reign of Charles II, all that successive parliaments had done in favour of Presbyterianism was undone. The synods, presbyteries and kirk sessions were suspended until they could be revived as bishops' courts. In 1661 an act was passed to compel attendance at church. Some three hundred ministers refused to agree to these measures. These so-called 'Covenanters' held their services in farm buildings, houses and in the open.

On the accession of William and Mary, in 1689, Protestantism was restored, and the majority of Skye's clergy took an oath of allegiance to the Crown. There was a revival of religious faith in the Highlands. Even the Church buildings were held in high veneration, and in many places as the congregation approached the building, they could be seen kneeling down at various points and praying. Being buried in the church building was the sincere wish of many people, and bones and skulls sometimes littered the floor, after they had been removed to make way for more recent burials.

Not everyone favoured the religion established by William and Mary. In the late 1690s, a vacancy arose at Snizort. A replacement was needed for the minister, Mr Donald MacQueen, who had 'silenc'd himselfe' rather than conform to the Presbyterian settlement finally established in Scotland.

Over much of the Hebrides, Episcopacy (associated with the Stuart cause) had the support of both the clergy and lay people. The more fervent Jacobites could not be expected to abandon even the Roman Catholic faith. In 1700 a law was passed for the 'Prevention of the Growth of Popery in the Highlands'. This act resulted in the less devout Protestants as well as the Catholics taking the side of the exiled house of Stuart.

Cill Chriosd, Strath Suardal

Ensuring complete religious adherence in an area such as Skye had many practical difficulties. People often had to walk twenty miles to attend church. The size of the parishes, and the difficulties in travelling overland, made it impossible for the clergy to give adequate attention to their scattered congregations. They delegated to catechists and schoolmasters, but even this was not enough to stop the increasing disillusionment with the Presbyterian Church. The inevitable outcome was that some clergymen lost heart, and many spent increasing time farming their lands.

By the first quarter of the nineteenth century, an evangelical movement, which had begun to affect parts of the Highland mainland in the last quarter of the eighteenth century, reached Skye. One of the new evangelists who came to Skye was John Farquharson. His most influential convert was a blind man, Donald Munro, who was born at Achtalean in the parish of Portree in 1773. He lost his eyesight at the age of fourteen through smallpox. As he grew up he became a master of the fiddle, but on turning to religion he saw music as his mortification.

On one occasion, while preaching, Munro called upon his listeners to show their renunciation of 'worldly pleasures' by bringing their musical instruments to the head of Loch Snizort on a certain day for a public burning. The response was overwhelming, and a mound of fiddles and bagpipes was set alight.

Munro never learned to read, but it was said that he could quote the Bible from beginning to end without a mistake, and that he would correct anyone that he heard misquoting.

Although the evangelical movement was at first confined to Trotternish, it soon spread to Duirinish and Bracadale, as many lay preachers took up the cause. The 'Men', as they were called, condemned all secular entertainment. Their appeal was largely to the 'common' people: most of the gentlemen and ministers found their preaching distasteful.

The difficulties faced by the Presbyterian Church in serving the scattered communities of Skye had not been much eased during the early nineteenth century, and were often referred to in the *New Statistical Account*, written by the ministers of each parish in the 1840s. The Revd Robert MacGregor of Kilmuir wrote that the area of Kilmaluag was so remote that the clergyman only held service there once every fourth Sunday. The Bracadale parish church at Loch Beag was fourteen miles from the south of the parish, and six miles from the north, and a missionary and a catechist served the more remote areas. The Revd MacKinnon of Strath complained that due to the distances involved, church attendance was 'much influenced by the state of the weather'.

Lord Cockburn, during a stay in Corry in 1841, described a typical Presbyterian congregation –

> I never saw a more respectable country congregation. There were about 350 present, all except Corry's party in the humblest rank. The men had almost all strong blue fisherman's jackets. The women, with only one exception, so far as I could observe, had on red tartan cloaks or shawls and clean mutches of snowy whiteness, with borders of many plies . . . There was not one child or very young person . . . Some of them had walked eight miles, and some sailed three.

Given the purely geographical problems faced by the Established Church on Skye, the evangelicals found it easy to make converts. Another factor which turned people to the evangelicals was the Church's apparent lack of concern for those who lost their land during the Clearances. The Presbyterian Church's ministers often owed their appointments to the landowners, and took their side. Some ministers

preached that the Clearances were God's retribution for the people's wickedness, and hinted that God's will was being done through the landlords.

But the people at last found a sympathetic voice with the evangelicals. Most of the lay preachers were from similar backgrounds and understood their problems. Many people turned to religion as their only consolation when separated from family and friends who had been shipped away. They were told that there was a better world to come, that the present world was only a 'vale of tears'. Resistance to the Clearances was probably weakened by these preachers.

Through the teachings of the evangelical lay preachers, the people of the north and west of Skye were ready for secession when the Disruption took place in 1843. While the moderates in the Church of Scotland had accepted the control of Parliament in the Established Church, the evangelicals did not believe that Parliament had a right to intervene in the affairs of the church. In 1843, over four hundred ministers, more than a third of those present, walked out of the General Assembly, abandoned their manses and churches, and formed the Free Church. All the ministers in Skye remained true to the old church, with two exceptions – the Revd Roderick MacLeod of Snizort, and Revd John Glass of Bracadale. Most of Skye's population, however, was eventually converted to the Free Church through their preaching.

For many years all the services of the Free Church had to be held in the open, as it was refused sites for building churches. In the 1840s the Fairy Bridge near Dunvegan was the scene for large gatherings of people listening to the preaching of Roderick MacLeod. As well as denouncing music and dancing he also denounced the Clearances which confined his popularity to the lower orders of society.

To overcome the problem of not having a church, the Free Church minister for the Small Isles, Revd Swanson, bought a small boat, the *Betsey*, which served as a floating manse. Hugh Miller, the geologist and writer, a friend of Swanson's, spent some time travelling with the minister. The boat usually moored off Eigg, but when the weather was stormy the *Betsey* would often put in to shore at Isleornsay in Sleat. Miller was on the boat one Sunday when Swanson preached at Isleornsay –

> The anchoring ground at Isle Ornsay was crowded with coasting vessels and fishing boats; and when the Sabbath came round, no inconsiderable portion of my friend's congregation was composed of sailors and fishermen. His text was appropriate – 'He bringeth them into their desired haven', and as his sea-craft and his theology alike were excellent, there were no incongruities in his allegory, and no defects in his mode of applying it, and the seamen were hugely delighted.

Eventually landlords began to accept the Free Church, and allowed churches to be built. The Free Church of Snizort was granted a site for a church in Uig, by the local landlord Major Fraser, after many years of open-air services. Other congregations had more trouble. Kilmuir, for example, did not receive a church until 1860.

The Free Church ministers condemned the ceilidh, as well as communal singing at work. The Sabbath was a day of rest, prayer and scriptures, and no work was done on that day.

Another branch of Scottish Presbyterianism emerged in 1892 when a group of Highland congregations seceded from the Free Church to form the Free Presbyterian Church. Free Presbyterianism had a great deal of support in some areas of Skye, notably Portree and Duirinish.

In 1900, the Free Church joined with the United Presbyterian Church forming the United Free Church (the United Presbyterians had come into being in 1847 with the union of two of the largest groups of eighteenth-century seceders). However, a minority of Free Church congregations refused to join and remained a separate church. Then, in 1929, the United Free Church and the Church of Scotland were reunited, leaving the Free Church and the Free Presbyterians, which still have large memberships on Skye today.

Church at Dunvegan

These quiet stones
rest in the known relationship each owns.
On angled arch and sturdy walls,
on lintelled door and window spaces,
surpassing peace, through countless prayers bestowed,
still falls,
embraces
the roofless holiness where chalice flowed
with life in Eucharistic sacrifice.
For faith remembered, grace desired,
hope inspired
these quiet stones suffice.

Lucy Sanderson Taylor
(writing of St John the Baptist's Church, Caroy)

Thatched cottage, Luib

WAY OF LIFE

EVERYDAY life among many of Skye's inhabitants would have changed little over the centuries, with a crofter of a hundred years ago using fishing and farming methods similar to those of prehistoric times. It is only within the last century that the island's traditional ways have been shaken by an encroaching 'modern' world.

Before the twentieth century, life on Skye was documented mainly in the accounts of travellers to the island. Many of these visitors were well-to-do gentlemen, used to the luxuries of the south, who invariable painted a rather gloomy picture of the average islander's lifestyle. To find a more unbiased view of life on Skye it is perhaps best to turn to sources such as the *Statistical Account* (1792–6) and the *New Statistical Account* (1845). These were descriptions of each parish on Skye, written by either a local minister or schoolmaster.

Skye had no proper roads in the early eighteenth century. The 'roads' that did exist were little more than tracks, used mainly for driving cattle to the southern markets. When Knox visited Skye in 1786 many of the inhabitants were employed in road-building programmes around the island, each party accompanied by a bagpiper.

Roads were generally considered a great benefit to the island, but one complaint was that they brought vagrants such as gipsies, rag men and tinsmiths. The minister of Strath complained in 1845 that these 'undesirables' introduced tea drinking, tobacco chewing and smoking, and he advocated the setting up of anti-tea and tobacco societies, believing that more money was being squandered on these articles than any 'intoxicating liquors'.

The only village of any great size on Skye prior to the eighteenth century was Portree. The town grew up largely as the result of the plans of Sir James Macdonald, eighth baronet of Sleat, and many of the present-day street names, such as Somerled Square, reflect Portree's Macdonald connections.

Sir James, who was born in 1741, was educated at Eton and Oxford and spent a number of years travelling the Continent with Topham Beauclerk and the philosopher, Adam Smith. On his return he set about improving his estate. One of his goals was to build a large village at Portree to encourage local industry and trade. Sir James also established a large school there.

None of the other villages on the island grew to the size of Portree. By the 1840s the village of Broadford, for example, consisted of one inn, a shop, a school, and a scatter of black houses. At the beginning of the nineteenth century Lord Macdonald had plans drawn up to create a village of similar size to Portree at Kyleakin, which he was going to call New Liverpool, but the plans were too ambitious and were never realised.

Over most of Skye the population was concentrated in small groups of houses which had grown up near areas of good land. By the late eighteenth century, there were two types of cottages – black houses, built of drystone with rubble cores and thatched with straw, and earthen-walled houses, covered with turfs.

The black houses had floors of clay or earth. A hole in the roof let out the smoke from the fire which was built on a raised hearth in the centre of the room. Light penetrated the cottages through this smoke hole, or through a purpose-built slit in the wall. At night artificial light was provided by a cruisgean, a small dish of seal or fish oil with a rush wick. The thatched roofs of the cottages were replaced every year, and the old thatch, saturated in soot, was spread on the land as a fertiliser.

In a report on the parish of Portree for the *New Statistical Account*, the Revd Coll MacDonald noted that the houses of the poorer tenants were smoky and filthy, with the people living under the same roof as their cattle. Some of the black houses were partitioned, the cattle living in the half nearest the door, and the family living in one or two rooms in the other half. Other houses had no dividing walls, but the portion of the house with the animals in it was a couple of feet below the floor level of the living quarters. Manure accumulated, but the peat smoke from the fire in the living portion of the cottage deodorised the air.

By the end of the nineteenth century the islanders had begun to build the so-called 'white houses', but it was not until this century that these outnumbered the black houses. White houses had cemented walls, glazed windows and wooden floors. When a white house was built on a croft, the old black house was often converted for use as a byre or store house.

The local gentry of Skye built larger, grander homes. Some of these houses were surrounded by well-maintained gardens. When John Knox, a representative of the British Society for Extending the Fisheries, visited Talisker House in 1786, he was impressed by the garden, which overflowed with fruit and vegetables, and also by the well-stocked cellar.

Previous to the nineteenth century almost all lands on Skye were held in common, or by 'runrig'. In each township, patches of land for growing oats and, by the latter years of the nineteenth century, potatoes and turnip, were assigned by lot. A new allocation was made every three years or so to ensure that everyone had a chance to farm the better plots. A portion of land was also set aside for the landless poor. As drainage was not undertaken in an organised way, cultivation was generally carried out in raised strips, called 'lazybeds'. Beds about six feet in width were divided from each other by a trough a foot deep and two feet wide, ensuring a dry bed for the growing crop.

Loch Varkasaig

Sheep, Glendale

Tilling was done by spade, the most common implement by the seventeenth century being the cas chrom or crooked spade. Ploughs were not commonly used on Skye until the mid-nineteenth century. In 1772 the traveller Thomas Pennant commented that ground being dug by eight men with spades on the side of Loch Bracadale could have been turned in the same time by a single plough.

Harvesting was also done by hand, usually by uprooting the whole plant. The ears were burned off the stalks and the straw used to thatch the cottages. In the late thirteenth century a law was passed forbidding private milling, and the people were ordered to send their grain to the district mill to be ground. In return the miller received a thirteenth of the ground grain. It is probable that this was not enforced very rigorously in Skye and that querns were still kept in every house.

Sheep and cows were the animals most commonly raised on Skye. There were also large numbers of goats and horses, but few pigs, as they were considered unlucky. The native sheep were the 'Caoraich Bheaga', small animals with fine white, grey, brown, or mottled wool and good mutton. Some of the sheep were milked, and gave about a pint a day. Southern breeds were introduced in the early nineteenth century, bringing new strains of ovine disease which drove the native sheep to extinction by the 1840s. The native cattle and horses were also small but sturdy, and were kept outside for most of the year.

Before dyke systems were established, the fixing of property boundaries was sometimes carried out in a rather cruel manner. Representatives from the adjoining townships met, and heaps of stones were piled up to mark the boundaries. When this had been done, two boys, one from each group, were beaten, so that they would not forget the scene of the argument.

Little land was enclosed, and keeping the animals clear of the growing crops was a labour-intensive job; compensation had to be paid for damage done to another man's lands. In the summer the animals were taken up to higher ground to graze. Usually it was the young women of the community who tended the animals. They lived in the hills for much of the summer, in shielings, small circular or rectangular huts with a smaller adjoining room which served as the dairy and store. The huts had a stone foundation but were built mostly of turf. During their stay in the hills, the women made a great deal of the butter and cheese for the winter months.

Around the beginning of the eighteenth century, the landlords began to divide their farms into lots or crofts, each being let to a family. This period also witnessed the institution of payment of rents in cash rather than in kind. As the tenants had no form of lease for their land, they could be moved at any time. The new system created other problems. When a son married, he was given a portion of his family's lot, and this subdivision eventually led to great poverty and overcrowding.

In the *New Statistical Account* for Sleat, the minister noted that there were five hundred families in the parish and that two hundred and twenty-five of these, about eleven hundred people, paid no rent at all, but got their subsistence from small plots of land given to them by the rent-payers, on which they grew potatoes. At this time, the government made no provision for the poor, who were supported largely by parochial funds and the charity of their neighbours. The mentally handicapped also lived on the charity of neighbours and relatives, and it was considered a religious duty to give them shelter.

Crofting was very much a hand to mouth existence, largely dependent on spells of good weather. At the beginning of the eighteenth century there were some very bad winters, 1715 and 1717 being particularly severe. The sea was said to have overflowed in parts of Trotternish, breaking down many houses. In 1719 Sir Donald Macdonald wrote to his agent in Edinburgh informing him that he had given his Trotternish tenants a temporary rebatement because of their hardships. Again, in 1772 and 1773, food was scarce, and the government sent oatmeal to Duirinish and other parishes.

Another bad year was 1835, beginning with a cold, wet spring. Sowing was late, and much of the seed did not germinate. Potatoes were planted, but many of them rotted in the ground. Before the crops that did grow could be harvested, they were flattened by the rain. Even the straw was of a poor quality, and many of the cattle became emaciated. A great number of families became destitute that year.

Very little was done by the tenants on Skye to improve their lands, mainly due to the fact that few of them had security of tenure. No enclosures were built and little large-scale drainage was carried out as this would enhance the value of the land and lead to higher rents. In 1753 a law was passed establishing the principle of lease-holding, and some of the larger farms in Skye were enclosed as a result. But the majority of the people remained 'tenants at will' who could still be moved without reason if another person offered higher rent for their land.

By the time of the Clearances, population pressure was severe. From 1755 to 1801, the population of Skye increased by an average of forty-six percent. In Portree parish, for example, this meant that the population grew from 1385 to 2246 in just forty-six years. A major reason for this increase was the introduction of the smallpox inoculation. Before this time, whole families were wiped out in epidemics.

All the writers of the *New Statistical Account* alluded to this remarkable population increase, and the widespread poverty which resulted. The minister for Bracadale wrote that when it was feared that a cholera epidemic was about to spread to the parish, a survey was carried out and 140 families were found to be so poor that they did not even own a change of clothes. Unfortunately, the people had no way of complaining of their predicament – the farming system had them at the mercy of the tacksman.

Oddly enough, some of Skye's ministers praised the landlords for transferring the poor to America and Canada. Portree parish's minister, for example, wrote, 'The highest praise is due to Lord MacDonald for his liberality in his beneficent and patriotic enterprise'. The Kilmuir minister saw a government system of emigration as the only solution to Skye's problems. It should be remembered that most of the ministers had personal interests in supporting the landlords, having been appointed by them. But given the situation, it is very probable that emigration did seem one of the few solutions. The minister of Strath himself sent three of his sons to America, and was intending to send a fourth.

The high rents of the nineteenth century forced some of the islanders to seek work outwith the croft – at least for part of the year. Young people were sometimes engaged as servants in the larger houses of the tacksmen and chiefs. When a young man in service married he was allowed to build a house on his master's land, was

Tractor, near Elgol

given land to cultivate, grazing for two cows, a dozen sheep and two horses, and a yearly allowance of shoes. Two days a week he was allowed to do his own farming. Thomas Pennant noted that in some houses there were as many as twenty servants.

Other islanders went south annually, after the potatoes were planted, to take any jobs which they could find. Many of the older men went fishing on the east coast in June, July and August, returning home for the harvest. Some of the young women went to the Lothians in the autumn to work at the harvest. The money that they made in the south was spent over the winter when there was seldom any source of income. The Duirinish minister complained in the *New Statistical Account* that some of the girls returned pregnant, and that their children grew up without being recognised by the church, unbaptised and uneducated, an outcast class.

Commercial trading in food and goods on Skye began in the mid-seventeenth century. Before that there were some limited opportunities for trade in fish, animal hides and wool. In 1580 a licence was obtained from the Crown for the setting up of a fair in Portree. The early markets attracted only people from the island and livestock and other goods such as linen and cheese were sold.

In the seventeenth century, the better-off farmers on the island began to trade black cattle in Lowland Scotland. The cattle were usually taken south in the autumn when they were in the best condition. Pennant described how the cattle were made to swim to the mainland across Kyle Rhea, at low tide. Six to twelve animals were tied together, a rope fastening the jaw of one animal to the tail of the one in front, with the first beast in the line being tied to the boat.

Trade in black cattle continued at a high level until the beginning of the nineteenth century. Three festivals were held each year in the parish of Portree, in May, June and November. The first two were for the sale of black cattle, and the third was for hiring servants and transacting business. Broadford also held three annual markets for the sale of black cattle and horses.

In 1786 John Knox, the fisheries official, visited the west coast of Scotland north of Oban to report on the state of fishing and agriculture. He expressed his disappointment that so much of the money obtained from cattle dealing was squandered in the cities of the south instead of being put back into developing the fishing industry, trade and agriculture in the island.

Skye's fish trade began in earnest in the seventeenth century. At first it was not in the hands of the locals, but was controlled by fishermen from the east coast of Scotland and Holland. Their relationships with the islanders were seldom good. Gradually the Skye locals began to take a more active part in the fishing trade, and in 1787 the British Fisheries Society acquired land in Waternish with the aim of establishing a centre for the fishing industry on Skye.

A purpose-built fishing village, Stein, consisting of a quay, stores and houses, was established. The venture was a failure, and was abandoned the following year with a loss of £1241. This was largely due to the high price of salt, which was 10/– per barrel, cured herring only fetching between 16/– and 19/– per barrel.

Over-fishing eventually led to the destruction of the industry on Skye by the mid-nineteenth century. The minister of Strath, in the *New Statistical Account*, wrote that whereas at one time sixty or seventy boats could have been filled in a few weeks, it was now unusual if one could be loaded in a whole season.

Fish for local households were sometimes caught in a 'cairidh', a weir of stones built to trap fish as the tide went out. There was one cairidh a quarter of a mile long on Loch Snizort, from which anyone could take fish. Most cairidhs were later broken down by landlords wishing to reserve the fishing for their paying tenants. Fish were preserved by salting, or by hanging them from the rafters of the house to be smoked.

The kelp industry reached its peak in the late eighteenth century. In 1790, for example, a hundred tons were produced in both Duirinish and Strath. In kelp-producing districts, a man, known as the 'buachaille cladaich', was appointed by the elders to report the presence of a wrack on the shore. He did this by raising a bundle of tangle on a pole and allowed nobody to begin collecting until all the workers were assembled.

Kelp was produced by burning the sun-dried seaweed in small pits, and the ashes – rich in potash and iodine – were gathered up, packed, and sent to the south to be used in the manufacture of glass, among other products.

It is probably true to say that traditional Scottish industries never really took hold on Skye. Attempts were made to open coal mines in two different parts of the parish of Portree, Braes and Camusban, in the nineteenth century, but the seam was thin and too difficult to work and the scheme was abandoned.

Peat was the main fuel on Skye, and the cutting of peats was a communal activity among the islanders. A bank was opened up and the peats sliced with a long spade. The slabs were then spread out to dry, and after a week or two piled in large heaps and carried home to be stacked for the winter.

Although there were some tradesmen in each parish, including weavers, tailors, and brogue-makers, the majority of islanders were for the most part self-sufficient. Clothing was made at home. Before the seventeenth century, the most common dress for men was the 'breacan-feile', a kilt and plaid combined in one length of cloth. It was worn over the shoulder and belted around the waist, with a shirt underneath. Gradually the wearing of trews became more common. Women wore the 'arasaid', a white cloak with only a few stripes of colour, which reached almost to the feet. Married women wore a 'coif', a close-fitting cap, while unmarried women wore the 'snood', a looser fitting band.

Wool was spun and woven into cloth by the women of the house, who used natural dyes to add colour. Dying was usually done in the open air. Layers of wool were placed in a large iron pot with the dye plant and some water, and the mixture boiled and stirred until the desired colour was reached. Bracken produced a dark turquoise colour, and heather, pale green. Another popular dye was crotal, a rust-coloured pigment obtained from lichen. It was believed that the lichen was always trying to get back to the rocks, and that anyone sailing in a jumper dyed with crotal would sink straight to the bottom of the sea if he fell overboard.

Waulking, the processing of the cloth once it had been removed from the loom, was also done by women. The cloth was soaked in urine and then pounded on a table to accelerate the thickening of the web.

Food for the majority of the islanders was produced locally. Martin Martin noted that very little meat was eaten, and that the early eighteenth-century diet consisted largely of cheese, milk, bread (made of oats or barley), butter and gruel. Potatoes, which became a staple in the diet by the end of the eighteenth century, were sometimes served with fish, but rarely with meat. In the winter, in times of hunger, cattle were occasionally bled, and the blood mixed with meal to make a kind of black pudding. Shellfish and seaweed were only eaten as a last resort.

A richer diet was enjoyed by the better-off. Purchases made in Glasgow on behalf of the Chief of MacLeod, in the last decades of the seventeenth century, included fruits such as prunes and raisins, various spices, sugar and wheat flour. Tea made one of its first appearances in the island in Roag in the early eighteenth century. A box of tea arrived from the East, sent from a sailor to his two old aunts. Unfortunately he forgot to say how the tea should be served, so the old ladies stewed the leaves, and topped them with butter!

Lobster Creels, Kyleakin

Jetsam

Smuggling of goods such as tea proved a constant headache for the authorities. In 1744, at a magistrates' meeting in Skye, the gentlemen present promised not to drink smuggled tea, and 'if it were humanly possible' to prevent their wives and daughters from doing so. But smuggling continued, and in 1829 a large boat with a cargo of tea, snuff, gin and tobacco was captured in Loch Snizort, along with a crew of eleven.

On his visit to Skye in 1773, Dr Johnson noted that those who could afford it had all the products he was used to in England – tea, coffee, butter, honey, conserves and marmalade – but he complained of the islanders' habit of eating cheese for breakfast.

Shed, Glen Sligachan

He observed that dinner differed little from that in England, apart from an over-reliance on milk puddings.

Wine drinking did not catch on in Skye until the mid-sixteenth century. Before then, a beverage called 'bland' was drunk. It was made from whisked whey left to ferment in cogs of wood for weeks. Wine enjoyed only a brief period of popularity among the islanders, being superseded by whisky, brandy and ale which had become available by the mid-seventeenth century. Most of the whisky was produced locally.

A distillery was established at Carbost in 1830. In the *New Statistical Account*, the minister of Bracadale listed three main changes which had taken place in the parish since the previous *Statistical Account* – the building of a road round the parish, the joining up of several smaller farms to form larger ones, and the erection of the whisky distillery. He felt that the first of these changes was of benefit to the parish, the second a disadvantage, and the third 'one of the greatest curses which, in the ordinary course of Providence, could befall it or any other place'.

Johnson noted that many Hebridean men started the day with a tot of whisky – perhaps to fight the cold. Indeed, most of the medical complaints of the islanders were put down to the moist, cold weather. Rheumatism, asthma, pneumonia, fevers and consumption were most common, but at times there were outbreaks of smallpox and other contagious diseases.

Martin Martin listed home remedies for various illnesses – dulse boiled and eaten with its infusion for colic; nettle tops chopped finely, mixed with the whites of raw eggs and applied to the forehead for insomnia; and a green turf heated beside the fire until hot and then applied to the side of the face, for toothache. The MacLeods of Dunvegan had their own doctors. The Beatons were their hereditary medicine men and were particularly noted for their skills with herbal cures.

Psychological illnesses were not neglected. Martin wrote of a smith in Kilmartin, well known for treating 'faintness of the spirits', or depression. The patient was laid on the smith's anvil, face upwards. The smith then took his hammer and swung it above his head, grimacing, before bringing it down with all his force, but stopping just before hitting the patient's head 'else he would be sure to cure the patient of all diseases'. The effectiveness of the 'cure' is left unreported.

Martin also listed various cures for sick animals. For example, when a cow was bitten by an adder, the affected area was washed with water which had been poured over the head of a dead snake. Snakes' heads were considered very precious and were preserved carefully. A quantity of wild sage chewed between the teeth and then put into the ears of cows or sheep which had gone blind was said to cure them. Two fossils common on Skye, ammonites and belemnites, were much used in animal healing. When a cow had cramps, the affected part was massaged with water in which ammonites or 'crampstones' had been steeped for hours. Belemnites were also steeped in water, which was then given to horses to drink as a treatment for worms.

Justice on the island was applied little more exactingly than early medical cures. Under the Lords of the Isles, individual chiefs were the judge and jury at a local level, and often interpreted justice to suit their own ambitions. A supreme court of appeal did exist in the Lord's Council, but this was of little use to the common man.

The last public execution on Skye took place in Portree in 1742. A travelling merchant was murdered at Rigg. Two men were convicted because a young boy witnessed the crime. He had been held by the murderers and made to swear that he would not tell a living soul what he had seen. But the experience weighed on the boy's conscience so much that he confessed to his minister that he knew something

terrible but could tell no one. The minister suggested that he confide his troubles to a nearby rock. The confession was overheard and the identity of the murderers established. One of them, Angus Buchan, was hanged at the gibbet in Portree.

Following the '45, the chiefs lost their prerogative to administer justice, and a sheriff-substitute for Inverness district was installed in the island. In the eighteenth century there seems to have been little serious crime, apart from sheep and cow stealing. Two families were banished from Duirinish for cow stealing in 1785. A few years earlier in Kilmuir, a man was found by two of his neighbours with a stolen sheep on his shoulders. He said it was his first offence and offered a reward if they would keep it quiet, but they declined. The sheep was set free and the man hanged himself from the roof of his house.

No jail existed on Skye until one was built in Portree in 1800. In the *New Statistical Account* the Revd MacDonald stated that the people were 'powerfully under the influence of moral principle, so much so, indeed, that heinous crimes are seldom or ever seen or heard of among them'. In the previous year the jail had been occupied by only sixteen offenders – eleven for riotous conduct, four for housebreaking and theft, and one for forgery. Revd MacDonald stated that the jail had been insecure for some time, and that various prisoners had broken out. Perhaps this is understandable as the jail had no beds or bedding and no fire. Only a small allowance was given to the prisoners for subsistence, and they depended largely on the charity of those living locally. Today the former Portree jail is the local Tourist Information Office.

The road to Claigan

Waterstein

CUSTOMS AND FOLKLORE

SKYE has a colourful population of mythical and supernatural characters, some kindly, some sinister. A rich story-telling tradition has breathed life into this miscellany of banshees and giants and wraiths and preserved them over the centuries.

Perhaps the most ubiquitous of all is the fairy. Skye's fairies vary in size from those as large as humans, to those small enough to get into a house through the tiniest of spaces. Fairies dress in similar clothes to humans (though often slightly out of date), and have similar possessions, borrowed or stolen from disorderly households. As well as Gaelic, they speak a strange fairy tongue, and are fond of music. Anyone who does the fairies a favour can look forward to a great deal of help in return, but those who cross them can expect to be paid back, sometimes in the subtlest of ways.

Fairies on Skye are said to keep cattle, red and speckled, and able to cross the sea. Fairy cows have the power to lead 'human' cows away through a rock or knoll unless intercepted, and the presence of a fairy cow in a herd of 'human' cattle can be detected by the restlessness and distressed lowing of the herd. There are only about ten spots in Skye where the fairy cows will graze, one being the Braes of Portree. It is reputed that when the cows come home to Braes from pasture, the following words can be heard, as the fairy woman counts her cattle –

> Crooked one, dun one,
> Little wing grizzled,
> Black cow, white cow,
> Little bull black-head,
> Mine milch kine have come home,
> Oh dear! That the herdsman would come!

Dunvegan Castle is well known for its tales of fairy magic. One of the most prized of the Castle's treasures is the 'fairy flag'. At the Castle Sir Walter Scott was told that when the flag was brought out in battle it increased the numbers of the MacLeods, if spread on the marriage bed it ensured fertility, and it could also bring herring into the loch.

Another tradition holds that the flag, unfurled, has the power to save the clan from destruction, but this power can only be evoked three times. Only one wave is thought to be left, which is just as well given the tattered state of the flag, now preserved under glass. On the third waving of the flag, the clan will either have complete victory over its foes, or will become extinct for ever. It is not a risk worth taking.

Various stories are told to explain how the flag came into the MacLeods' possession. One is that an early chief fell in love with and married a fairy, on the promise that their life together would last for no more than twenty years. On the day she left him, at a spot now known as 'Fairy Bridge', she dropped part of her silken clothes as she flew away, and these were picked up and kept by the chief. The more probable explanation is that the flag was brought back from the east when one of the chiefs was on a crusade.

Skye fairies are fond of stealing children. One day, the wife of the tacksman of Rudh' an Dunain was having a rest while her neighbour minded her baby daughter by the fire. The heat from the fire made the neighbour drowsy, and soon she was sleeping too. After a while the mother looked over at the fire and saw three fairies gathered round the baby. One was encouraging the others to carry off the infant,

Skye

while another objected, saying that they should leave the baby as they had already taken so many of the woman's children, and the third fairy agreed. But the first fairy, angry at being outvoted, vowed that when the peat on the hearth had burnt out, the child would die.

As soon as they had gone, the mother got up and poured a bucket of water on the fire. She took the damp peat, wrapped it up and placed it in a casket. Years later, the daughter became engaged. It was the custom in those days that the bride-to-be did not attend church between her engagement and marriage. One Sunday, while her mother and father were at church, the girl decided to look inside the casket which her mother had guarded so carefully over the years. On forcing it open she was surprised to find only a little piece of peat and she tossed it onto the fire.

As the peat burned, the girl began to feel ill, and by the time her parents had returned from church, she was almost dead. Her mother could find the peat nowhere among the scattered contents of the casket. The girl died and was buried at Eynort.

Rather more conspicuous than the fairies were the giants. One famous giant was Cuchullin, the Ulster hero, who came to Skye, so the tale goes, to attend a school for warriors set up by Skiach, a great female fighter. Cuchullin took only three strides to reach the hills of Skye, and on his arrival challenged the other students to single combat. All were defeated. Skiach gave him permission to fight her daughter, an honour usually withheld until the second year of study. The pair fought for a day and a night and another day before Cuchullin won.

Skiach was outraged and descended from her seat on top of the hills to fight Cuchullin. For four days and nights they battled without a victor. Eventually the daughter persuaded them to stop and eat. They realised that neither would ever win, and made peace, promising that if one needed the other's help, it would be forthcoming. Cuchullin returned to Ireland, and by the time he left, Skiach respected him so much that she called the Skye mountains where they had fought Cuchullin's Hills.

Glendale is another of the areas associated with the giants. It was here, in the fertile pastures, that they fed their grey goats and their cow Glas Ghoillean (Grey Shoulders). The cow gave eleven gallons of milk at each milking, and could speak. While chewing the cud she had time to produce many Gaelic proverbs.

Many of the Skye communities had a 'gruagach' (long-haired one), a rather nasty character which cast spells on cattle, lessening their yields. The gruagach could be placated with gifts, such as an offering of milk placed in a hollowed out stone, the 'gruagach stone' of the district.

Another of Skye's more sinister creatures is the luideag, an odd, goblin-like creature, with two arms but only one leg with a cloven hoof. A luideag was said to live between Loch nan Dubhrachan and Broadford, in a dark moorland valley scattered with marshes and many small lochs. At nightfall he could be seen hopping from dry patch to dry patch on his one leg. Any traveller unfortunate enough to be met by the luideag ran the risk of being beaten around the head or knocked into a pool.

Most feared of Skye's mythical creatures was the water-horse. Unlike the luideag who was easily recognised by his one leg and ragged clothes, the water-horse could disguise itself as a human or an ordinary horse, beckoning people to the loch where they were devoured.

Often the water-horse appeared as a handsome young man, desirable to innocent young women. Only the seaweed and sand caught up in their hair gave them away, but by the time a woman made this discovery it was often too late to escape.

One water-horse was said to have disguised himself as an old woman to try to trap some girls staying at a shieling on the slopes of Beinn a'Sgà near Loch Snizort Beag in

90

Trotternish. The girls had just gone to sleep on their large bed of heather when there was a knock at the door. An old woman stood there, asking for a place to sleep. She would only agree to sleep in the centre of the bed, as she was afraid of the water-horse.

After an hour or two the girl nearest the door felt a movement, and turning round saw the old woman with her teeth in the arm of the girl beside her. She ran outside, pursued by the water-horse which had assumed its own form once more, and jumped over a small stream just as the cock was crowing thus saving herself from the water-horse, who could not cross running water during the day.

The water-horse was not just a phantom made up to scare young women into moral rectitude; islanders believed the creature truly existed. In the late 1800s an organised attempt was made to catch the water-horse said to live in Loch nan Dubhrachen. On the day that it was to be caught, a holiday was declared, and a picnic organised. Two boats with a net stretched out between them dragged the loch. During this process, the net caught in a rock and the spectators, fearing that any minute the water-horse would be brought to the surface, ran from the scene. All that the net contained was two pike.

As well as the water-horses, Skye also had water-bulls, 'Tarbh Uisge'. One lived off Flodigarry island. Any slit-eared calf was thought to have been fathered by a water-bull, and was killed at once.

Numerous sightings of sea serpents have been reported around Skye. In 1808 a minister called Donald MacLean spotted a monster-like creature with an oval head and broad shoulders, tapering to a thin tail.

One mythical beast which seems to be unique to Skye is the 'Biasd na Srogaig', or the 'beast of the lowering horn', a large clumsy animal with long legs, and one horn. If nothing else, the threat of it kept children quiet. An equally frightening beast, an Uraisg, lived in Coire-nan-Uraisg, the Corrie of the Monster. Just the sight of this apparition, half human, half beast, with shaggy hair, fangs, and long curved claws, was enough to destroy a man.

Not all 'sightings' of apparitions were imaginary, as this story, which appeared in *The Clarion of Skye* for July 1955, demonstrates –

The Italian's Monkey

In 1890 a strange Italian arrived in Glendale, Skye, carrying a large box on his back. He came to the Schoolhouse and offered to show us, for a penny from each scholar, a beautiful monkey. Our schoolmaster explained to him that his pupils were poor and that they had no pennies but at the same time he offered the Italian 2/– if he would show us the monkey. This offer the Italian refused. He then lifted the box on to his back and went away talking to himself, no doubt cursing the school and the schoolmaster. That night he got permission from a crofter at Uiginish to stay in his barn, monkey and all. During the night the monkey went scouting around and finally arrived at a cottage occupied by an old maid, and finding the kitchen window open, he went inside and took possession. About 1 a.m. the Maid was surprised to hear someone prowling about in her kitchen. She immediately got out of bed and armed herself with a hay-fork and went to investigate. When she opened the kitchen door, here indeed was, which she believed, the Devil himself, standing on the table and wearing her Sunday hat and doing his toilet. The Maid did not wait another second but plunged the hay-fork right through his breast and the monkey died instantly.

Customs and Folklore

91

The Storr

The gallant maid then put the Devil in a bag, still wearing her best hat, and with the help of Patty's lantern, she buried him in her garden. She kept the secret to herself for a whole year and when she died she left £4 in her will to the Italian for the loss of his monkey in Skye. Also the following letter, which is a copy of the original: 'Dear Mr Italian, it was me that killed your monkey. I thought at the time it was the Devil himself. I was very sorry for what I did and I am leaving you £4; it will help you to get another monkey'. – M.M.L.

The Italian was found in Florence, Italy, and the £4 was very much appreciated by him.

Skye, like most parts of Scotland, has its ghost stories. Often the ghosts in these tales were known to the people that they haunted, and were not always terrifying, though usually a nuisance. In the east of Skye, around 1800, a man died leaving only his wife to look after the croft. One of her chores was to watch the cows in case they left their pen and trampled the growing crops.

One night she had to leave her task for a while, and some of the cattle got out. When she returned, her late husband was there minding the herd, and telling her not to worry. Every night after that he was there watching the animals. This was more than the woman could take, and she decided to sell up and emigrate to America. On the day of the sale, it was impossible to gather the cattle which seemed terrified of a little bird hovering about them. The sale and the move were abandoned, but from that day on, the ghost's visits stopped.

Ghosts do not always haunt alone. At Duntulm Castle, on misty evenings, a procession of armed warriors can sometimes be seen, all dressed in the kilts of their clans, and ready for war. They are said to be the ghosts of the many killed during battles around the castle walls.

Skye has also had its share of witches. Legend holds that they could assume many guises such as cats and whales, and had a wide range of powers including the ability to induce storms and inflict disease.

Witches on Skye were prosecuted right up until 1880. The last known case was in Uig where an elder of the Free Church accused a mother and her five daughters of taking milk from a neighbour's cow by 'evil arts'. They were not burnt.

Three witches said to live at Camustianavaig, near Portree, set themselves up as consultants for evil deeds. One of their clients was the skipper of a local boat who wished to get even with a rival crew. He went to consult the witches one night while his boat was harboured at Portree, bringing a bottle of whisky. Only two of the witches were at home, but they decided to go ahead with the business rather than wait for the third witch to return.

By the time they had decided on a suitable spell, the whisky bottle was empty. As the skipper was leaving to rejoin his boat, the third witch returned home. She was furious when she found out that not only had the discussion taken place without her, but also that there was no whisky left for her. She would not be pacified. The following evening all was calm, but as the skipper's boat was sailing past Camustianavaig, a squall suddenly blew up, enveloping the boat and the crew. It is said that the wind often gusts at Camustianavaig, even on the calmest of days.

Witches were believed to possess 'the evil eye', and were blamed for such deeds as charming the milk away from cows. They carried out their evil at night, sometimes taking the form of an animal such as a hare. If, while in this guise, a dog attacked them, they retained their injuries even after being restored to their human form.

Various methods were used to reverse the actions of the evil eye. One was for the owner of the charmed stock to walk about the district from house to house, showing the occupants the affected milk, in the belief that the damage could be undone if the evil eye looked on it again.

A less harmful, but generally unwanted power was that of second sight, said to be more rarely found today because people have lost contact with nature. Second sight can take various forms, but is usually connected with foreseeing death.

One story is told of a minister who, while on a visit to Portree, was caught in a storm and had to take shelter at a house in Scorrybreck. The lady of the house went into the attic for something, and minutes later the family and the minister heard her scream. She eventually calmed down enough to recount what had happened. The parish cloth for covering coffins was kept in her attic, and the woman related that she had seen it light up with the image of the minister's niece. Soon the girl became ill and died, the first death in the parish since the incident in the attic.

Sometimes those about to die were not recognisable to the person with second sight. One woman saw a spectral funeral procession passing along the side of a hill. There was no road following the route which it took. After the woman died, a boat

Overleaf:
Storm over the
Sound of Sleat

went down in the loch beside the hill, and the bodies were later carried along the hillside where she had seen the funeral procession.

A sure sign of death was the apparent shrinking in size of a person, followed by their recovery to normal size. A tacksman of Feorlig, accompanied by his servant, saw the minister of Duirinish passing one day. The minister shrank to the size of a boy of six before growing back to his former size. He soon grew sick and died.

Revd MacGregor of Kilmuir, writing in the *New Statistical Account*, reported that four people in his parish admitted to having second sight. The signs of death they spoke of were blue quivering lights moving along the route of a funeral procession, or around the bed in which someone was about to die.

Seers also practised their arts on Skye. One was Coinneach Odhar who told the fortunes of various families on the island. An uncanny prediction was made for the MacLeods of Dunvegan. Kenneth prophesied that: 'when Norman, the son of a slim English lady, died accidentally; when the 'Maidens' (the rock stacks off Uiginish Point) became the property of a Campbell; when a fox had a litter in one of the turrets in the castle; and when the fairy flag was brought out for the last time, a great part of the MacLeod lands would be sold off, but that a chief named Iain Breac would later repossess the lost estates, and raise the esteem of the house to a higher position than before'.

A Dr Norman MacLeod, visiting Dunvegan Castle in 1799, witnessed the first part of this prophecy fulfilled. He had gone to watch the castle smith force open the casket containing the fairy flag. News was then received at the castle that Norman, the MacLeod heir, had been killed when his ship, the HMS *Queen Charlotte*, was blown up. The 'Maidens' were sold off at this time, to an Angus Campbell, and a fox in the turret of the castle had a litter which Dr MacLeod picked up and handled.

Although many preferred to leave the supernatural well alone, there were others who dabbled in 'taghairm', contacting the spirits. In the eighteenth century this was usually done by a combination of isolation and fasting by the person who was to receive the message. When Thomas Pennant visited Skye, he came across this practice in Trotternish. A man had been dressed in cowhide and placed in a hollow behind a waterfall. Pennant was unconvinced, despite the fact that the man appeared to go into a trance and foamed a bit at the mouth.

Many customs and superstitions were intricately woven into the day-to-day activities of the islanders. The two big festivals of the year were Beltane in the spring, and Samhainn in the autumn. At Beltane the herds were put to pasture and the crops were sown. Special bannocks were baked and the girls washed their faces in the dew at dawn to attain beauty.

At Samhainn the herds were brought into shelter and the crops were harvested. At both festivals, all household fires were put out and rekindled from bonfires blazing on 'the hill'. Any fire not rekindled with this 'fire of god' was considered unlucky and unholy. This rite continued in some parts until the nineteenth century.

Martin Martin, writing in the eighteenth century, noted that the natives still observed the influence of the moon. They dug peats in the decrease, as peats dug on the increase were thought never to dry out. Timber was felled and rushes cut on the decrease. Earthen dykes built on the increase of the moon were sure to fall. Planting was done when the moon was new.

Numerous other rituals were carried out to bring good fortune. To safeguard cattle from disease they were encircled with burning torches; this was thought to be most effective at Whitsuntide. Similar treatment was given to growing crops.

Wild animals and birds had their place in superstitious belief. This rhyme lists some sightings considered unlucky –

Chunnaic mi clacharan air gàrradh toll,
Chunnaic mi seilcheag air lic bha lòm,
Chunnaic mi eun-ghabhrag air mullach tom
Chuala mi chuthag's gun biadh 'nam bhrionn
Chunnaic mi searrach 's a chulaobh rium
'S dh'aithnich mi nach rachadh a' bhliadhna sin leam

I saw a stone-chitter on a broken dyke,
I saw a snail on a bare ledge
I saw a snipe on the top of a grass tuft.
I heard the cuckoo before having food,
I saw a foal with his back to me,
and I knew the year to me would not be a prosperous one.

Allt Coire nan Bruadaran,
by the head of Loch Ainort

Some places, such as the well at Loch Shiant, were held to have sacred properties. Sick people bathed in the loch, drank its water and also made offerings by dropping in trinkets and strips of coloured cloth, in the belief that they were drowning the spirit of their disease.

Skye, like other areas of Scotland, has a variety of customs associated with birth, marriage and death. Unbaptised babies were always in danger of being kidnapped by fairies, who would leave one of their own children in their place. These 'changelings' were constant sources of trouble. Precautions were taken before a baby was baptised, to safeguard it from this fate. Someone walked around the mother and baby with a burning peat, seven times in the morning, and seven times at night, a charm guaranteed to keep the baby safe.

On the morning before a baptism, bread was baked, and served out to people on the way to the church. If the baptism was a multiple one, the boys were always first in line, because it was said that if a girl was baptised first, she would grow a beard when she was older. The ceremony of purification was carried out on returning to the house, when the baby was passed from mother to father, seven times, over a basket of bread hung to the pot-chain.

Before the mid-seventeenth century, 'handfasting', rather than a church wedding, was common. The couple lived together for a year and a day, and if they got on well the marriage was legally binding. If they did not get on, the contract was dissolved. Any children from the handfasting period had to be maintained by the father.

After the mid-seventeenth century, handfasting still went on, but most marriages were conducted in church. When a man wanted a girl's hand in marriage, he went to her parents' house with his father and a few friends. Once at the door of the girl's house, the oldest in the party asked if the girl would marry the man who wanted her hand. If this was agreed, the man's party entered the house and had a drink to celebrate. This was the 'An Còrdadh Beag', the 'Little Agreement'.

About two weeks later came the 'An Réiteach Mór', the 'Great Contract'. At this meeting the wedding plans were made, and the date of the marriage and amount of the dowry fixed. Only Tuesdays and Thursdays in the waxing moon were lucky days for the marriage. About a week before the wedding, the couple walked round the village inviting friends and relatives. The wedding presents were food and drink for the celebrations which usually lasted for a few days. At night there was music, singing and dancing, and games during the day.

On the morning of the wedding, the friends of the bride gathered at her home, the friends of the groom at his. They were entertained at the respective households, and it was not until after the ceremony that the two parties joined.

At the end of the celebrations the couple were accompanied to their new home. The guests paired off and formed a procession, walking to the accompaniment of the pipes, or singing. When they arrived at the house, the oldest person in the group broke a bannock over the bride's head as she crossed the threshold. It was lucky to catch a piece of this bannock.

On the morning after the wedding, the bride's mother went into the bedroom and put the bride's hair into a pointed linen coif before she left her bed. The new wife was helped to dress by her female friends, and when this was done they marched out of the bedroom in a line headed by the bride. The first man to meet the girls on leaving the bedroom had to spontaneously address the new wife in verse – the 'poet's blessing'.

By the nineteenth century, marriage had lost much of the ceremony, traditions and fun attached to it. This was due to widespread poverty, and also to the teaching of the evangelicals. Only a few close relations and friends now took part in the celebrations.

In the 1920s and 1930s it was common for every house in a village to have a candle burning in each window as a welcome to the wedding party. But on funeral days all the houses along the way of the procession kept their curtains closed until the mourners had passed.

Until recently, when someone died, all work was stopped until after the funeral, as a mark of respect. If there was any perishable food in the house of the dead person, a piece of iron was inserted into it, otherwise it was believed that the food would decay at the same time as the body. Two containers were placed on the chest of the corpse once it had been laid out – one contained salt representing the imperishable soul, the other contained earth representing the mortal body. Neighbours watched the body by turns, and much eating, drinking and dancing accompanied this 'wake'. The coffin was carried to the burial ground, followed by the women wailing and singing to ensure rest for the soul. Immediately after the interment, the mourners began to drink round the graveside. Much of this stopped in the nineteenth century.

The bodies of suicides were not taken from the house by the door, but were passed through an opening made between the wall and the thatch. Suicides were usually buried outside the wall of the burial ground, along with unbaptised children. It was believed that no fish could be caught in any stretch of water which could be seen from a suicide's grave.

ARTS AND EDUCATION

BEFORE the late eighteenth century there were no schools on Skye, and formal education was largely restricted to the children of the better-off. The local gentry formed organisations to employ teachers, often very well educated men. One was Martin Martin, the author of *A Description of the Western Isles* and a noted scholar of the classics. These teachers were paid very little.

Although an act was passed by the Scottish Parliament in 1696 instructing every parish to establish a school and build a school house, none was built on Skye in compliance with the act. Education was not totally neglected, however. The Society for the Propagation of Christian Knowledge, formed in 1709, soon made its influence felt on Skye. The Society ran classes on the island only during the winter months as most of the children were needed to work on the crofts for the rest of the year. A barn or byre, or any other kind of shelter that could be found, served as the classroom.

By the time that Johnson and Boswell visited Skye in the 1770s, parish schools had been built in a number of areas, including Sleat and Strath. Sir James Macdonald's school in Portree was in operation, educating children from all parts of the island.

Johnson was appalled by the extent to which the islanders' native tongue was neglected. 'Their language is attacked on every side. Schools are erected, in which English only is taught, and there were lately some who thought it reasonable to refuse them a version of the holy scriptures, that they might have no monument of their mother-tongue.'

Enough schools had been built to serve most parts of the island by the mid-nineteenth century. However, schools faced problems on a similar scale to churches when it came to ensuring attendance. Distance was a problem in some areas, as in Portree parish where, although there were two parish schools, a school run by a society in Glasgow, and two Gaelic schools, all were inaccessible to children from Braes and Glenmore. Crofting families also found it difficult to afford the nominal fees. In Kilmuir parish, the minister put the poor attendance at the school down to the inability of the parents to properly clothe their children and purchase books. Parochial and Society schools taught a variety of subjects including English and arithmetic, but the Gaelic Society Schools confined their teaching to Gaelic.

Despite a lack of formal education, the islanders were not uncultured. There was a rich tradition of music, poetry and story-telling, and in the absence of television and radio, the ceilidh (a gathering of friends and neighbours for singing, playing the fiddle and pipes, and reciting), was the main source of entertainment in the community.

Much of the traditional music and song of the island was lost when the playing of the pipes was banned after the '45, and later in the nineteenth century when the evangelicals preached against playing music and singing. But enough fragments of poetry and music survive to show that Skye's early chiefs were great patrons of the arts. Often a castle would be home to all or some of a bard, piper, fiddler and harpist.

The bards were held in high regard by medieval Gaelic society. Qualifying as a professional bard required that the rules of poetry be memorised, along with many poems and tales, a long and difficult training. Three hundred and fifty such poems and tales had to be committed to memory in order to qualify for the highest degree of bardship.

Bards were often equally adept at composition. Most of the tales they composed concerned heroism and great warriors, and the glory of battle. Hints of their brilliance survive in the Ossianic ballads, the popular form of strictly metred poems, the subject matter of which dates back to as early as the ninth century. Their fiery inspiration eventually led to a clause in the 'Regulations for Chiefs' forbidding the patronage of bards and advocating their punishment in the stocks.

By the seventeenth century the 'Orain Mhóra' or 'Great Songs' of the 'vernacular poets' began to supplant the ballads of the earlier bards. Many of the 'Orain Mhóra' praise the chiefs, patrons of the bards, and are composed using stressed metre, more like modern poetry.

The earliest examples of this metred poetry to survive, with the exception of a couple of pieces, are by Mary MacLeod of Skye and Iain Macdonald (Iain Lom) of Lochaber, both seventeenth-century poets and both completely untrained in bardship. Although Mary MacLeod has been described as 'the inimitable poetess' of the Isles, there is no evidence that she could read or write. It is generally believed that the work of these two poets is too perfect for either of them to have originated the style.

Mary MacLeod, or Màiri Nighean Alasdair Ruaidh (Mary, daughter of red haired Alasdair), is believed to have been born in Rodel, Harris, around 1615. She did not begin to compose until relatively late in life, while employed as a nurse by the MacLeods of Dunvegan. At some point she composed a song which upset her chief so much that he banished her to Mull. While exiled, Mary composed 'Luinneag Mhic Leòid', (MacLeods' Lilt) which so touched the chief that he forgave her. Mary is said to have had a bad ear for music, and another woman is thought to have composed the tunes for her songs.

One of Mary's songs, 'Cumha Mhic Leoid', was sung at the bedside of her chief, one of the MacLeods of Dunvegan. Pretending he was sick and dying, he had Mary summoned to the bedside and told her he wanted to hear the lament she would compose for him. The first part is as follows –

Mo chràdhghal bochd
Mar a thà mi nochd
Is mi gun tàmh gun fhois gun sunnd.

Gun sùrd ri stàth
Gun dùil ri bhith slàn,
Chaidh mo shùgradh gu bràth air chùl.

Chaill mo shusbaint a càil.
Fàth mo thùrsaidh gach là,
Is mi sìor-ursgeul air gnàths mo rùin.

Mu dheagh mhac Ruairidh nan long,
Lamh lìobhraigeadh bhonn,
Is bha measail air fonn luchd-ciuil.

Sad and heart-sore my weeping,
for I find myself tonight without rest,
without peace, without cheer;

With no will for aught that profiteth,
without hope to be well;
my joy is vanished for ever more.

My substance hath waxed listless,
cause of my grief each day,
as ever I recount the ways of my dear one;

My grief for Roderick's son of galleys,
his a hand to lavish wealth,
who esteemed the minstrel's lay.

Highland music also has a long tradition. Bagpipes were probably invented independently in many countries, and there is no need to suppose that the instrument was introduced to Scotland from outside. The earliest pipes had one drone. A second drone was introduced around 1500, and a third one added later. In Scotland, compositions for the pipes, the piobaireachd or pibroch, were very highly structured. There are three main types of piobaireachd – the salute, the gathering, and the lament.

The office of piper to a Highland chief was hereditary. Most famous of the piping and composing families on Skye are the MacCrimmons, who were pipers to the MacLeods of Dunvegan. The first MacCrimmon to hold this position was Iain Odhar ('the Dun' – probably because of sallow complexion). He was patronised by Alasdair Crotach who assigned the district of Boreraig rent-free to the family, on condition that they trained one of their sons for the office of piper to the clan.

Although there is no record of any composition by him, it is likely that he passed on his knowledge to his son Donald Mor who probably lived between 1570 and 1640, and composed a number of piobaireachd including *The MacLeod's Salute*.

The MacCrimmons founded a piping school at Boreraig. The founder was probably Patrick Og, who became official piper to the MacLeods around 1730. Patrick was a great teacher, player and composer, and the founders of most of the great piping schools studied under him. A piper's course at Boreraig lasted three years and each pupil had to memorise 195 compositions of Ceol Mor ('great music') before qualifying as a master.

Among Patrick Og's pupils was Charles MacArthur, founder of the MacArthur school and tradition of piping. The MacArthurs became the hereditary pipers to the Macdonalds of Sleat. One of their better known pieces is *Lady Macdonald's Lament*, composed by Angus MacArthur.

Until quite recently, pipers were all taught exclusively from canntaireachd. The master would sing the phrase to be learned, then the pupils played it back on their practice chanters.

On the death of Sir Rory Mór, thirteenth chief of the MacLeods of Dunvegan, Patrick Mór MacCrimmon composed one of the finest laments in song, the *Lament for Rory Mór MacLeod*, a 'pibroch' song. It is impossible to say if the words or the music were written first.

Tog orm mo phìob	Give me my bagpipe
Is théid mi dhachaigh	And I will go home
Is duil-ich leam fhéin	There is grief within me
mo léir mar thach-air	Seeing what has happened
Tog orm mo phìob	Give me my bagpipe
's mi air mo chràdh	Anguished as I am
Mu Ru-air-idh Mór	Over Ruairidh Mór
Mu Ru-air-idh Mór	Over Ruairidh Mór

Traditionally pipers went into battle at the head of their clan. *Cha Till mi Tuille* (*MacCrimmon will never Return*), better known as *MacCrimmons Lament*, is a pibroch song composed by Donald Ban MacCrimmon on leaving Dunvegan Castle to oppose Prince Charles in the '45. The piper had a premonition of his own death and believed he would never again see Dunvegan. Indeed he was killed by the first shot fired on the MacLeods as they neared the Prince's headquarters at Moy Castle. The incident inspired Sir Walter Scott to write a poem about the piper's departure from Dunvegan Castle –

MacLeod's wizard flag from the grey castle sallies,
The rowers are seated, unmoor'd are the galleys;
Gleam war-axe and broadsword, clang target and quiver,
As Maccrimmon plays 'Farewell to Dunvegan for ever'

Farewell to each cliff, on which breakers are foaming,
Farewell each dark glen in which red deer are roaming,
Farewell lonely Skye, to lake, mountain and river,
MacLeod may return, but Maccrimmon shall never.

Farewell the bright clouds that on Culen are sleeping;
Farewell the bright eyes, in the fort that are weeping;
To each minstrel delusion farewell! and for ever –
Maccrimmon departs to return to you never.

The Banshee's wild voice sings the death dirge before me,
And the pall of the dead for a mantle hangs o'er me;
But my heart shall not fly, and my nerve shall not quiver,
Though devoted I go – to return again never!

Too oft shall the note of Maccrimmon's bewailing,
Be heard when the Gael on their exile are sailing;
Dear land! to the shores whence unwilling we sever.
Return, Return, Return, we shall never!

There is now a museum of piping in Boreraig, and a beehive cairn nearby, built as a memorial to the school of piping, has a plaque which reads –

The Memorial Cairn of the MacCrimmons of whom ten generations were the hereditary pipers of MacLeod and who were renowned as Composers, Performers and Instructors of the classical music of the bagpipe. Near to this post stood the MacCrimmons School of Music, 1500–1800.

The MacLeods still retain their links with piping. A yearly competition, the Silver Chanter, a masters' event, is held at Dunvegan Castle, attracting some of the world's top pipers.

The MacArthurs, pipers to the Macdonalds of Skye, originally came from Mull or Islay. They occupied Hunglader in Kilmuir rent free until 1776. Angus, the last of the MacArthurs, died in 1800. He is buried in Kilmuir churchyard. The stone slab marking his grave reads –

> Here lyes the remains of Charles MacKarter whose fame as an honest man and remarkable piper will survive this generation for his manners were easy and regular as his music and thus tho the melody of his fingers will . . .

The inscription ends mid-sentence, and there are two explanations – firstly, that the mason went on strike because he felt he was underpaid, and secondly, that the son of MacArthur was lost at sea while the stone was being chiselled and that the mason abandoned his work when he heard the news, believing it unlikely that he would be paid.

In 1746, the bagpipe was held to be an 'instrument of war', and was banned. However, the ban was not the only cause of the instrument's decline. As the chiefs took up the lifestyle of the south, the piper's position in the household declined along with the clan system.

Another leading instrument of medieval Gaelic society was the harp, the oldest of Scotland's three national instruments (harp, pipes and fiddle). Poetry was sometimes recited to a harp accompaniment. Only one harper rivals the MacCrimmons in importance – Roderick Morison, better known as Ruaidhri Dall (Blind Rory) or as An Clarsair Dall (the blind harper).

Morison was born in Lewis around 1660. While training for the church he contracted smallpox and lost his sight. Morison then gave up the ministry and went to Ireland for harping tuition. On his return to Scotland he met Iain Breac, sixteenth Chief of the MacLeods, who offered him the post of family harper. Morison stayed at Dunvegan until Iain Breac died in 1693. The next chief, Roderick, dispensed with the position of family harper and Morison had to give up his 'harper lands' at Claggan.

No compositions for the harp can be directly attributed to Morison, though it is probable that some of his work exists in traditional music.

Scots fiddle playing in its finest form is usually associated with the North-east of Scotland, but the West, particularly Skye, had some famous fiddlers. These included Lachlan McKinnon (Lachlunn Mac Thearlaich Oig), a seventeenth-century bard and fiddler, and Neil Campbell Macintyre of Sleat (Neil Mór). Skye fiddlers drew their inspiration from the music of the pipes, producing a style distinctive to that of the North-east.

A great proportion of Skye's traditional Gaelic songs which survive are in the form of labour songs. There are two main groups – songs for communal tasks, in which strong rhythm helped the workers to synchronise their movements; and songs to lighten the lonely work of the women around the house or while milking. A vast collection of these labour songs was made by Frances Tolmie, born in 1840 at Uiginish Farm. She had no recording equipment, and wrote down the songs and tunes as she heard them.

Songs to accompany the waulking of cloth are the most common of the communal songs. Most of those which survive seem to date from the mid-sixteenth or seventeenth century, but the tunes are probably far older.

Waulking was a method of thickening and softening newly woven cloth. A waulking table was set up in a barn or shed, or in the open. The cloth to be worked was soaked in urine diluted with hot water – a simple domestic ammonia, which fixed the dye, and made the wool soft.

The women sat at the table, round which the cloth was laid out. They would pound the cloth with their hands, and after every few beats, simultaneously tossed the area of cloth they were working to their neighbour. The singing was kept going by the 'leader' who was seated at one side of the table, but did not touch the cloth herself. At first she sang a phrase or two of a slow song, choosing her beat to match the pounding of the saturated cloth. As the moisture evaporated, the cloth grew lighter and the songs became quicker and more light-hearted. It took about half an hour to 'waulk' a piece of cloth, in which time about nine songs could be sung.

Waulking songs comprised a solo verse, usually only one line, often followed by a refrain of meaningless words, then a chorus, in which everyone joined in. The following is a waulking song remembered by Frances Bassin from her childhood in Minginish.

Loch Coruisk

Skye

Chaidh nas fir a Sgath-abh-aig
Fà-ill ill, O-ho-ró!
Tha'n là'n diu fuar ac'.
O hì ho-rionn o-hó

Chorus–
Hi ri ri ho-ro gù
Fàill ill O-ho-ró
Chaidh fear mo thighe-s' ann;
Fà-ill ill, O-ho-ró!
Caol mhala gun ghruaman
O hì ho-rionn o-hó.

Sealgair 'an ròin teillich thu;
Fà-ill ill, O-ho-ró!
Is na h–eilide ruaidhe;
O hì ho-rionn o-hó

Is na circeige duinne thu,
Fà-ill ill, O-ho-ró!
Nì a nead's a luachair
O hì ho-rionn o-hó

The men have gone to Scavaig
Fà-ill ill, O-ho-ró!
for them this day is cold
O hì ho-rionn o-hó

Hi ri ri ho-ro gù
Fàill ill O-ho-ró

The goodman of my house went there;
Fà-ill ill, O-ho-ró!
he of the slender eyebrows, showing no frown
O hì ho-rionn o-hó

Hunter of the bulb-cheeked seal art thou
Fà-ill ill, O-ho-ró!
And of the red hind.
O hì ho-rionn o-hó

and of the little brown hen
Fà-ill ill, O-ho-ró!
that makes her nest among the rushes
O hì ho-rionn o-hó

Sgurr nan Gillean

Other tasks accompanied by song would have included rowing and reaping, but it is often difficult to match the songs with specific tasks, as it was the rhythm rather than the words which was important. Rowing songs, for example, were probably also used as lullabies.

The dominant theme of Gaelic song and poetry by the nineteenth century was the Clearances. On Skye, the most famous poet to write of the cruelty of the time was Màiri Mhór nan Oran (Great Mary of the Songs) who was born in Skeabost in 1821. Mary left the island in 1848, after her marriage, and lived in Inverness. Although a frequent visitor to Skye, she did not come back to live there until 1882, the year of Braes and Glendale. Màiri Mhór nan Oran was fifty years old before she wrote her first song in 1872. The following is an extract from one of her songs, 'Eilean a' Cheo' (The Isle of Mist), in which she expressed her hope that those who had been exiled, or their descendants would return in the future –

Ach có aig am bheil cluasan	Who can hear
No crìdh tha gluasad beò,	And has a heart that beats,
Nach seinneadh leam an duan so	That would not sing with me
Mu 'n truaighe 'thàinig oirnn!	About the misery that came upon us!
Na mìltean a chaidh fhuadach	The thousands that were banished
Thar chuain gun chuid 's gun chòir.	Over seas without means or justice.
Tha miann an crìdh 's an smuaintean	The desire of their hearts and thoughts
Air Eilean uain' a' cheo.	Are on the green Isle of Mist.
Nis, cuimhnichibh ur cruadal,	Now remember your distress,
'Us cumaibh suas ur stròil;	And keep up your hopes;
Gu'n tid an roth mué 'n cuairt duibh	The wheel will go round
Le neart 'us cruas nan dòrn;	With strength and vigour in its shaft;
Gu'm bi bhur crodh air buailtean	Your cattle will be in the fold
'S gach tuathanach air dòigh;	And every farm in good order;
'S na Sas'nnaich air am fuadach	And the English banished
A Eilean uain' a' cheò.	From the green Isle of Mist.

Another poet who has written passionately about the Clearances is Sorley MacLean, who has been described as one of the greatest Gaelic poets. He was born in 1911 on Raasay, but has Skye ancestry, and now lives in Braes, Portree. His mother's family had lived in Braes when it was cleared between 1852 and 1854, and the events were recounted to him by some of the older members of the family when he was young.

Very little prose has come out of Skye, perhaps not surprisingly given the island's oral tradition. Some writers such as Sir Walter Scott were, however, influenced by their visits to the island. Scott's impressions, formed over two visits, one on the Lighthouse Boat, provided the background for his poem *The Lord of the Isles*.

Another literary figure to write about Skye was Alexander Smith, the poet and essayist. He married a Skyewoman, Flora, and spent six weeks in Skye in 1864 when he stayed in Ord House in Sleat and later wove his experiences into the lyrical masterpiece, *A Summer in Skye*. He died of typhoid fever three years later at the age of thirty-six. In this extract of his book he recreates the beauty of the area near to his father-in-law's house –

Beyond the blue of the sea the great hills rise, with a radiant vapour flowing over their crests. Immediately to the left a spur of high ground runs out to the sea edge – the flat top smooth and green as a billiard table, the sheep feeding on it white as billiard balls – and at the foot of this spur of rock a number of huts are collected. They are half lost in an azure veil of smoke, I can smell the peculiar odour of peat-reek, I can see the nets lying out on the grass to dry, I can hear the voices of children. Immediately above and behind the huts and the spur of high ground, the hills fall back, the whole breast of it shaggy with birch-wood; and just at the top there is a clearing and a streak of white stony road, leading into some other region as solitary and beautiful as the one in which I am at present . . .

The Cuillin Hills from Strath Suardal

The Cuillin Hills from The Bad Step

Glamaig

FLORA AND FAUNA

SKYE'S flora and fauna is in many respects comparable to that of the rest of the Highlands and Islands of Western Scotland, but it does stand out on several counts. Among other things Skye can boast the highest breeding density of golden eagles in Britain, forty percent of the world's grey seals, a more diverse flora than any other area of a similar size in Western Europe, and a midge season which is infamous worldwide.

Few people make the climb to the 'alpine habitat' on the upper slopes and ridges of the Cuillin Hills. This is the island's least hospitable environment – the extreme weather and lack of soil mean that little can survive apart from a few grasses and lichens. Further down, many of the steeper slopes are covered with extensive screes, again supporting little or no vegetation. Starry saxifrage and Alpine thrift grow in small crevices in the rocks, out of the wind. However, in a corrie of the Black Cuillin Hills, a rare plant known as *Arabis alpina*, or alpine rock cress, thrives. It is found nowhere else in Britain.

Alpine plants such as mossy saxifrage, purple saxifrage and roseroot grow in the Quiraing and the Storr, also the habitat of another plant rare to Britain, the Icelandic purslane (*Koenigia islandica*).

The treeless mountainous areas of Skye are the haunt of the ptarmigan and the golden eagle. The ptarmigan is a small gamebird, grey and white except in winter when it turns almost totally white. Its wings are short and it has a heavy flight. Often the ptarmigan does not make a nest but lays its eggs in a slight hollow.

The golden eagle is large but graceful with a wingspan of between thirty and thirty-five inches, the female having a slightly larger span than the male. The eyries are large, made of twigs and sticks, heather and grass, and are usually built high in the crags. Golden eagles feed mainly on small mammals such as rabbits and mice as well as on carrion. They have been known to take small lambs, and consequently many have in the past been hunted out by sheep farmers worried about their flocks. Now both the birds and their eggs have special protection.

Red and roe deer inhabit some of the more remote glens of Skye. Red deer are the larger of the two, and have antlers up to 3 feet in length. In summer their coats are reddish brown with white below, and in winter brown with darker brown below. Roe deer have red-gold coats in summer, and brown ones in winter, when the males have a white patch under the throat. Red deer often live in herds, whereas the roe deer live in much smaller groups.

The underlying geology of an area greatly affects its flora. The Red Hills, for example, have very acidic soils unsuitable for many plants but home to bog myrtle, mosses, ferns, and liverwort, whereas the limestone pavements of Strath provide an environment in which small ferns, grassland herbs, and plants such as mountain avens and yellow saxifrage flourish.

On grassy banks and in open meadow areas, a wide assortment of wild flowers including primroses, the deep yellow lesser celandine and purple dog violets bloom in the spring. A bit later blue wild hyacinths flower, followed by foxgloves and dog roses (mainly dark pink). Three kinds of St John's Wort (perennial herbs with five-petalled yellow flowers) grow on the island. In Gaelic St John's Wort is known as 'Achlaisean Challum Chille', the armpit package of St Columba. Islanders sometimes carried the plant as a charm to counteract witchcraft, and would put it in the bottom of a pail before milking to improve the yield.

Overleaf:
Broadford Bay

Much of the basalt regions of the north of Skye have poorly drained peaty soils with a bog vegetation. Three types of heather flourish in these areas, and flower from late June to September. The first to flower is the cross-leaved heath which has four leaves in a cross formation and rose-pink flowers. Next to bloom is bell heather, which has a crimson-purple or, more rarely, a white flower, followed by ling or true heather which has pink or 'lucky' white flowers. In the past, heather was used to fill mattresses and for thatching.

Although from a distance these peaty areas may seem totally dominated by heather, a rich variety of plants and flowers can be found on closer inspection. These include the tormentil which has yellow flowers, and eyebright, a small relation of the foxglove, which has pink or white flowers. There is also heath bedstraw which was used to scent bedding, and cotton grass (or bog cotton), often thought to indicate dangerous marshy ground. Bog cotton used to be spun like flax, and was also used to fill pillows.

More rare are the orchids, among them the heath spotted orchid, the marsh orchid and the lesser butterfly orchid. Insectivorous plants include the butterwort (*Pinguicula vulgaris*) which has a ring of thick leaves with sticky hairs that fold round unsuspecting insects. The plant flowers purple in the summer.

Open moorland areas are the hunting grounds of the kestrel, sparrowhawk, merlin, peregrine falcon and buzzard, where their prey includes hare, shrews (pigmy, common and water), house and field mice, short tailed and bank voles, rats, rabbits, weasels and stoats. The kite ceased to breed in Skye near the end of the nineteenth century.

Moles are confined to the Edinbane and Bernisdale areas. They were introduced into Skye by Lord Napier of Magdala. Some escaped and there is a population bounded by the Skeabost River. In Samuel Johnson's time there were no rats on Skye, but the eminent scholar complained that weasels were so common that they were regularly heard in the houses rattling round behind chests and beds.

Wolves were exterminated in Skye in the 1740s. Wildcats, although still found on the island last century, are now extinct. Despite various attempts to rid Skye of foxes, they still survive. In 1774 the landlords imposed a tax of 'fox money' on their tenants. This money was collected along with the rent and then shared out at the end of the year to those who had killed foxes. In 1765, a hundred and nineteen foxes were killed in Trotternish alone.

The bracken and heather found on the moorlands, in combination with the damp weather, provide ideal conditions for Skye's midges. The biting season is June, July and August when the female midge needs a blood meal to lay a full quota of eggs. The Revd John MacCulloch, visiting Skye in the early 1800s, described the midges as 'the torment of this country', and related his frustration at not being safe from them even when anchored offshore in the Sound of Soay –

> That their teeth are sharp, is too well known, and I can answer for the goodness of their noses. We had anchored about a mile and a half from the shore; yet they scented us; and in about a quarter of an hour, the vessel was covered with this 'light militia of the lower sky'. Considering that the animal is barely visible, his nose cannot be very large: let philosophers, who explain every thing, determine how an odoriferous particle could be projected for a mile and a half, to hit full butt on an olfactory nerve, of which ten thousand might stand, like the schoolmen's angels, on the point of a needle . . . There are not many things more ingenious than the snout of a midge.

Balmeanach

Reptiles are rare on the island. Slow-worms, a legless variety of lizard (also called blindworms because their eyelids close after death), live on the island, feeding on worms, caterpillars and slugs, and hibernating in burrows in autumn and winter. There are some adders, most often seen in the remote heathery areas. Revd Channcey Hare Townsend who visited Skye in the mid 1800s, related his encounter with an adder while walking in the Cuillin Hills –

The only living thing that I saw in these mountain fastnesses was a huge viper, lying partly coiled up on a knoll close to the path-side, and which erected its head and brandished its quivering forky tongue just as if it meant to make a dart at us. Had our guide seen it, he would doubtless have tried to kill it; but, as he passed it without notice, I said nothing to call his attention that way . . .

The heathery areas provide cover for a variety of gamebirds including snipe, woodcock, pheasant and red grouse. There are many smaller birds resident on Skye and found in most of the lower ground – the sparrow, wren, stonechat, blue tit, yellowhammer, linnet, reed bunting, pied wagtail, blackbird and thrush to name but a few.

House martins, wheatears, tree pippits, skylarks and cuckoos migrate to the island in the summer. Tradition has it that when a MacLeod chief died all the cuckoos would leave Skye to take news of the death to the MacLeod subjects in St Kilda, and that the inhabitants of that island would be found in mourning by the time the MacLeod messenger arrived.

In marshy areas and along river banks, herons can often be seen, standing still in the water, watching for fish or frogs. Of the island's ducks, the mallard is most conspicuous. The golden eye is a common winter visitor, while the pintail, teal and tufted duck nest only occasionally on Skye.

Other migratory birds include the barnacle goose, the Greenland white-footed goose, the great northern diver and the whooper swan. Whooper swans have a black bill with a yellow base, and take their name from the call they make in flight. Before 1824 when Loch Chaluim Chille was drained for land reclamation, it was frequented yearly by large flocks of these swans which appeared on 25th October regularly, and stayed for five months. Hundreds could be seen at once. The autumn after the draining, the swans arrived as usual, but as recorded by the minister of Kilmuir parish in the *New Statistical Account*, 'on observing the destruction of their favourite haunt, they hovered with a cry of sadness for a brief period over it, then disappeared, and have seldom been seen since near the place'.

The lochs and boggy areas of Skye have their own distinct flora. Around the edges of lochs, the white or pink flowers of bogbean or buckbean can be seen in May. In folklore these flowers are the living trace of fallen angels. Rushes grow on the wet parts of the moor, and around lochs. When oil lamps were used, the outer skin of the rushes was peeled off and the pith used as wicks. In the lochs themselves, water-lilies are found – the white ones being much more common than the yellow. The roots, cut with a special hook, were at one time used to produce a black dye. Flag or yellow iris, flowering through spring and summer, is another common 'marsh' plant.

Nobody knows exactly how many otters there are on Skye, but they can be spotted along many of Skye's rivers, and along the coast. At Kylerhea an otter haven has been established by the Forestry Commission. The Highlands and Shetland are the last otter strongholds in the world.

In Skye's rivers and fresh water lochs, fishermen can catch brown trout, salmon, Arctic char, rainbow trout (an introduced species), three-spined stickleback, flounder and brook lamprey. Some of the freshwater lochs contain eels, Loch Mor in Waterstein being best known. The following letter was sent to the *Clarion of Skye* in February 1953 in response to a query as to the lack of trout in the loch.

About 23 years ago, when I was on University vacation, a companion and I were having an exploratory ramble on the shore below the Bita Mor. We came to the 'eas' or waterfall of 30 feet or thereabout, which drains the loch, and there in front of us was one of the ugliest sights imaginable. Two mammoth heaps of moribund and seemingly dead black-eels – many of them six to ten feet in length and the girth of an average sized oar. They were piled four or five feet high. As there had been heavy rain with the wee burns in spate during the preceding day or two, we presumed that the overflow had flushed out of the loch several hundreds of those black, ugly creatures.

Skye was once well-forested. Evidence from pollen studies suggests that in post-glacial times, the island was thick with birch, alder, hazel, and a small number of elm and oak. About 5,000 BC the climate got wetter, and the woodlands declined. Much of their destruction, however, has been due to man, clearing the forests for timber to build houses and to make space for crop cultivation. Tradition holds that all of Trotternish was once a forest which was burnt down by the Norse.

Remnants of the old woods still stood at Portree and Sleat when the *Statistical Account* was written in 1792. By the time that the *New Statistical Account* was written in 1845, some 460 hectares of mixed conifers and broadleaves were thriving through coppicing and planting, mainly in Strath and Sleat, but also in Portree and Kilmuir. Imports of cheap timber and the agricultural depression of the 1880s led to the neglect of these plantations, and the mature timber was exported.

Today, the commonest areas of natural woodland are the sheltered pockets in the south of the island, for example in Sleat. Tokavaig Wood, in southern Sleat, is one of the few remaining natural ash woods, also containing bird cherry and hawthorn. Coille Thochabhaig, a site located within Tokavaig Wood, contains eighty-one hectares of ash and hazel woodland and has been designated the status of a National Nature Reserve (Skye's only one) by the Nature Conservancy Council. Here a broadleaved woodland of native species survives along with one of the richest areas in Scotland for 'Atlantic' bryophytes. Parts of the woodland are fenced off in rotation to encourage regeneration.

The basalt areas of the north and west of Skye support only small patches of hazel scrub, birch and alder, with isolated rowans and aspen. Outwith this area there are few trees. In the eighteenth century there were no trees in Dunvegan, but in the last decade of the century, General MacLeod began tree planting. Unfortunately, thousands of these trees were blown down in the storms of 1921.

Skye's coastline varies from the exposed and remote cliffs of the north of Skye to the flatter beaches of the Broadford and Kyleakin areas. Numerous species of sea birds inhabit the cliffs around the coast, among them the oystercatcher, fulmar, tern, shag, kittiwake and Arctic tern. Martin Martin recorded that on the south side of Loch Portree there was a large cave in which many cormorants nested. The natives were interested in catching them to eat, as it was said that the young birds made good soup. To catch the birds a fire of straw was made at the entrance to the cave once it was dark, and the birds flew to the light, being caught in baskets as they reached the opening to the cave. Puffins are occasionally seen, but usually inhabit the smaller offshore islands where they breed.

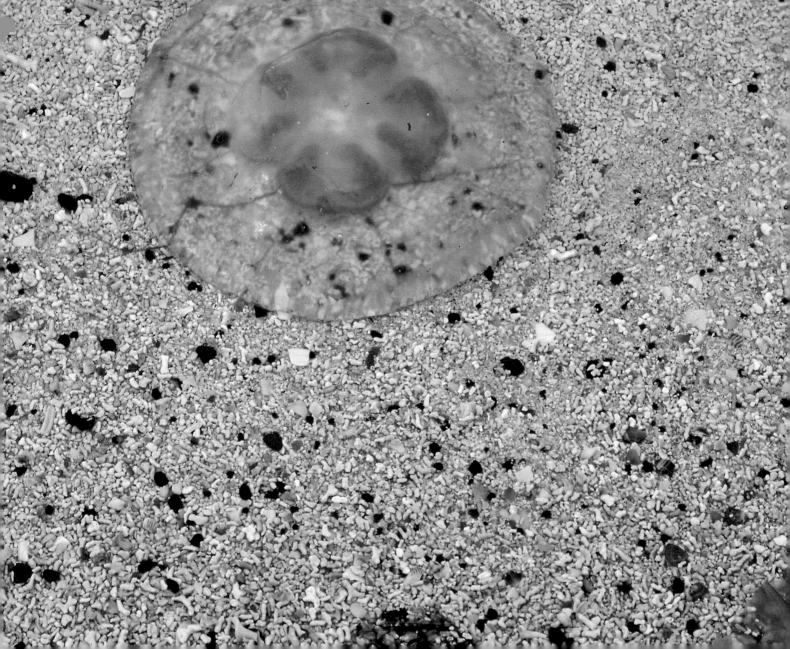
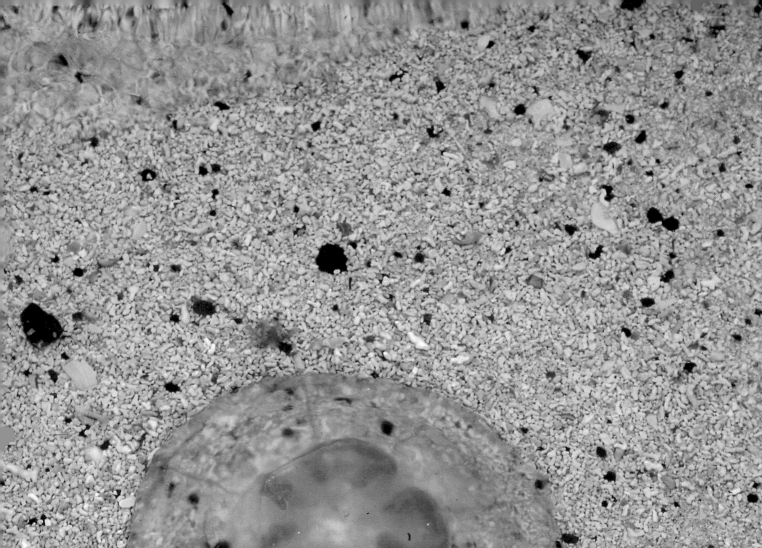

Hunting eradicated the white-tailed or sea eagle from Skye by the beginning of the twentieth century. However, sea eagles were reintroduced into Rhum from Norway several years ago, and there is now evidence that they are once more breeding in Skye. They are Europe's largest eagle with a wing span of up to seven feet ten inches.

Few would consider Skye's famous 'Coral sands' near Dunvegan a part of the island's 'flora', yet the 'coral' is actually formed from a plant, the red alga *Lithothamniun calcareum*. It takes on its coral structure when the calcareous 'skeleton' of the alga is bleached white by the sun. A similar beach can be found near Broadford. Martin Martin noted that a quantity of the red coral with an egg added to it was a good cure for diarrhoea.

Shellfish, their shells forming some of Skye's beaches, include limpets, razor fish, oysters, clams and mussels. Among the commonest sea fish around Skye are the cod, haddock, herring, mackerel and whiting, but there are dogfish, wrasse, turbot, ray and skate in lesser numbers.

The largest fish in Skye waters is the basking shark (*Cetorhinus maximus*), which can grow up to 40 feet in length. In 1945, Gavin Maxwell, author of *Ring of Bright Water*, set up a fishery for basking sharks on the island of Soay, off the south-west coast of Skye. Maxwell, in his first book *Harpoon at a Venture*, described his first encounter with a basking shark –

> At first it was no more than a ripple with a dark centre. The centre became a small triangle, black and shiny, with a slight forward movement, leaving a light wake in the still water. The triangle grew until I was looking at a huge fin, a yard high and as long at the base. It seemed monstrous, this great black sail, the only visible thing upon limitless miles of pallid water. A few seconds later the notched tip of a second fin appeared some twenty feet astern of the first, moving in a leisurely way from side to side . . . I could only guess at what was beneath the surface.

The sharks were harpooned out in the Minch and then taken back to the factory on Soay to be dissected. Maxwell's venture ran into financial difficulties and folded in 1949, but even if it had not, it would probably have failed eventually, through over-fishing, as basking sharks are very slow to reproduce.

Whales have been seen in Skye waters – porpoises, killer (orca) whales, dolphins, pilot whales and minke whales being recognised. In the past, when a whale was beached, the islanders would remove its teeth and blubber.

There are around thirteen hundred common seals resident in the more sheltered lochs and sounds around Skye. Seals were at one time killed for their fat, skin and flesh. Now they are an important tourist attraction though not always popular with fish farmers. Grey seals are larger than common seals and prefer the more exposed coasts and remote islands. Occasionally spotted in the waters around Skye, the grey seals do not have breeding grounds on the island, but breed on the offshore islands such as the Ascribs and Raasay.

Skye may appear to be a wildlife haven, but several species of bird and animal are under threat from various quarters. The seal population is one such case. Although the common seal is legally protected from being killed, the grey seal is only protected for part of the year. The increase in fish farming poses a possible threat to the seal population. A fish farmer is allowed to legally shoot seals if they are presenting a threat to his stock. The problem is that it is up to a fish farmer to decide when a seal poses a threat, and there is little independent policing of the waters.

Fish farmers will sometimes kill otters and birds such as herons, cormorants and shags. Some put up preditation netting, but this is costly. Wild fish in the lochs may also be under indirect threat from fish farming, and various studies are being carried out on the problem. The build up of food and faeces from the tanks is thought to threaten the natural environment of the wild fish.

Another area of controversy is increased afforestation, which may be a threat to some birds of prey. Forty to forty-five pairs of golden eagle breed on Skye. If forestry proposals go ahead, some believe that Skye could lose between eight and twelve pairs due to tree planting in their hunting grounds.

Wildlife issues on Skye are the special concern of Andrew Currie, the regional representative of the Nature Conservancy Council. Currie, who has held the job for fifteen years, spends much of his time persuading landowners, farmers and crofters to take an interest in conservation. To protect unique habitats the NCC has the power to designate Sites of Special Scientific Interest (SSSIs). Once areas are protected, applications have to be made to develop them. In Skye there are between fifty and sixty SSSIs, two thirds of them being geological. Others are botanical, for example, one takes in a group of lochs in the Sligachan area which supports the pipewort, an American plant. Nobody knows how it got there.

Paul and Grace Yoxon of the Broadford Field Centre are also deeply concerned with the protection of Skye's natural heritage. The centre was set up in 1985. As well as recording data on otters, seals, dolphins, porpoises, whales and basking sharks, the Yoxons take in injured animals and birds. In 1988, during the seal virus outbreak, they set up a seal rescue unit in the centre. Fortunately, there were only a couple of cases of the virus on Skye, and the tanks are now used for the treatment of injured, orphaned or abandoned seals.

Paul Yoxon feels that the whole of Skye is a 'special site'. Rather than instituting 'panic conservation' when a species of plant or animal is about to disappear from an area, he believes that conservation should be an ongoing process. But his is only one voice. The preservation of Skye's wildlife depends on the value placed on it by the whole community – farmers, developers, visitors and government alike.

Loch Dunvegan

DOL DHACHAIGH–2	GOING HOME–2
seall na geòidh	see the geese
a' siubhal 's	journeying and
na gobhlain-gaoithe	the swallows
's fhad' o dh'fhalbh a' chuthag	long since the cuckoo went
seall na duilleagan dearg ag	see the red leaves
éirigh air	rising on
sgiath sgairt-ghaoth	the wing of a gust
ag éirigh 's a' siubhal	rising and travelling
tha'm bradan sgrìob mhór a-mach	the salmon is a great way out
air a shlighe	on his journey
ghrian a' dol 'na sìneadh	the sun reclining
ghealach ag éirigh	moon rising
'nam parabolathan caochlaideach èolach	in their familiar changing parabolas
samhradh a' siubhal	summer journeying
foghar air a dhruim	autumn on his back
cleòc mór a' sgaoileadh as a dheidh	a great cloak spreading behind
null 's a-nall air cala	back and forward on the wharf
fògarrach a-null 's a-null	an exile back and forward
null 's a-nall	back and forward
null 's a-nall	back and forward

Aonghas Macneacail

TWENTIETH CENTURY SKYE

SKYE entered the twentieth century with a population much in decline, an enduring effect of the Clearances. Bracadale, one of the areas most affected by the Clearances, had a population of 2,103 in 1821 but by 1921 the number had declined to 740. Today, the average population per square mile in Skye is twelve, compared with a UK average of 567.

The decline of the population and the failure of the kelp and fishing industries had gradually become issues of national interest by the late 1800s. However, 'The Highland Problem' was exacerbated by the unwillingness or inability of government to tackle the situation. In the years between the two World Wars, many islanders were forced to find work in the industrial belt, settling in areas such as Clydeside.

The World Wars also brought about short-term shifts in the population of Skye, when the men of the island were called into service. Although Skye seemed far removed from the battle fields of Europe, day-to-day life was significantly altered. In many households the women were left to run the crofts single-handed or only with the help of children and older family members. During the First World War there was an added hardship as much of the ploughing had to be done without the use of ponies, all except the white ones having been appropriated for the war effort.

Skye was affected more directly by the Second World War. German U-boats patrolled the waters around the island and convoys of Allied ships could be seen sailing through the Minch on their way to America and Canada. Skye was within a restricted area north of the Caledonian Canal, and passports were needed to enter or leave the island. Refugees, mainly children, were transported to Skye to escape the bombing raids along the Clyde and in other parts of southern Scotland.

The rebuilding of Britain's economy after the Second World War meant little to the average Highland family. Many of the pre-War hardships remained. As Fraser Darling, author of a report on the Highlands and Islands in the 1950s put it – 'Had Britain been physically three parts Highland, the problem would not have arisen, because the nation would have developed with this particular environment as a major part of its being, instead of as a sore little finger'.

In 1965 a government agency was set up by an Act of Parliament to deal exclusively with the problems of the North. The Highlands and Islands Development Board was given a substantial budget, along with a remit to bring the North of Scotland into step with the economic and social development of the nation.

In Skye grants have been given for industry and tourism as well as for croft improvements and sports facilities. One of the latest ventures on the island with HIDB backing is the Staffin Community Co-op which has a hall, restaurant and shop.

Skye's depopulation underwent a reverse during the 1970s, largely due to the attractions of the island to the retired and to young immigrants looking for an 'alternative' lifestyle. Since then the island's population has shown a steady increase, from 7,364 in 1971, to 8,495 in 1988. Twenty-five percent of the population of Skye is over retiral age, due mainly to people who left Skye in their younger days returning to retire, and the continuing drain of young people to the mainland in their search for work.

'Incomers' to the island have not always been welcome. The majority of them are from England, the north as well as the south, but there are also families from other parts of Scotland, and from abroad. Among other things they have been blamed for pushing house prices out of the range of local people. However, many of the incomers are enthusiastic in adopting Skye's traditions, including Gaelic.

Overleaf
Portree

The Kozikowski family, Orbost House

The Skye ferry at Kyle of Lochalsh

One such incomer is George Kozikowski, a medical microbiologist who sold up in London and moved to Orbost House near Dunvegan with his wife Sandy and their two children. The Kozikowskis run a guest house and their oldest child attends the local school where she is learning Gaelic. Like many of those settling in Skye, the Kozikowskis sought to escape the frustrations of city life: the nine to five routine, commuting and the lack of accessible countryside. On Skye they hope to find a more traditional lifestyle centred about a small community.

Although crofting has declined markedly on Skye, the scattered crofting townships remain the basis of the settlement pattern on the island. Subsidies are available to encourage the raising of livestock; in 1986 almost 170,000 sheep and 6,000 cattle were kept on Skye. Agricultural development on any grand scale is constrained by the climate and land, along with the costs of transporting freight to the island.

A croft is now defined as a piece of land of less than seventy-five acres, with an annual rent of less than £50. A crofter can pass the tenancy to an heir or assign it to a stranger, with the approval of the Crofters Commission. Crofters now have the option of buying their croft for a comparatively small sum, but few have done so. In 1969 the census showed that 106,000 acres were owned in Skye and 183,000 rented.

Under the EEC, crofting has become increasingly regulated. The Scottish Crofters Union has been formed to ensure that the voice of the crofters is heard when decisions affecting their livelihood are made in Brussels.

In February 1989 Skye had an unemployment rate of 18.7 percent, compared to a Scottish average of 10.5 percent. Unemployment figures usually drop in the summer due to seasonal employment in the hotel trade. About 600,000 tourists visit Skye every year, housed by a varied collection of over seventy hotels and guest houses, and a couple of hundred registered bed and breakfast establishments. This is not including the growing number of holiday cottages for rent. The hotel trade provided some four hundred jobs in June 1977, a quarter of all on the island. However, not all of these go to locals, many jobs being filled by students and seasonal workers from other parts of Britain.

Tourism has by no means provided a solution to the 'Highland Problem', as much as successive governments have liked to believe. Many believe that more effort should be put in to attracting industry to the island, providing a more stable base to the economy.

Various attempts have been made to provide year-round employment in the past century. In 1910 Dr Barbour of Bonskied built a basket factory to provide employment for crofters' children. He had hoped that local demand would absorb the factory's output of waste paper baskets, trays and other products. However, the cost of production proved too high to allow competition on the open market.

Skye's diatomite deposits once supported an industry providing work for between twenty and thirty people. The diatomite was transported by a small railway from Loch Cuithir to Inver Tote where it was dried and shipped. Production was stopped between the Wars, and no one has yet proved that revival of the industry would be profitable.

Just after the First World War a weaving-crofting community was set up at Portnalong on the shores of Loch Harport. People were moved to Skye from overpopulated areas in Lewis, Harris and Scalpay, and were given land and cows. They brought their looms, and the weaving sheds can still be seen outside many of the houses. A yearly sale of cloth was held at the village up until 1939.

Many of the islanders who still work their crofts on Skye do so only on a part-time basis, and supplement their income by such diverse means as taking in bed and breakfasters, running a shop or post-office, working on the roads, or supplying the craft outlets on the island.

Other industries on Skye include the Talisker distillery in Carbost, a sand and gravel quarry at Kyleakin, and a factory manufacturing medical instruments at Dunvegan, their highly specialised personnel being trained on the island.

Fishing still provides some employment, with shell-fishing being the most important. Fish farming – salmon, mussels, oysters and scallops – is on the increase, and there is a great deal of concern as to its effect on the natural aqua-environment. In general it is considered good for the island, creating employment. What worries some is the speed at which the industry has grown. Fish farming now employs almost as many people as traditional sea fishing. In 1986 there were 75 full-time fishermen, 32 part-time and 20 crofter-fishermen based on Skye (excluding Sleat), with fish farms employing 70 full-timers and 20 part-timers.

Forestry is gradually changing large areas of Skye's landscape, although the industry provides only a small amount of employment. Concern has been mounting over how many more acres can be planted before potential crofting land is lost. The tree most often planted now in Skye is the Sitka Spruce which will not grow on land above about 850 feet, and is not indigenous to Scotland or any of its islands. Controversy rages on the subject.

Compared with mainland Britain, Skye has always been slow to obtain its services and utilities. This time lag is usually due to the expense and distance involved in supplying the island. Television, for example, did not reach Skye until March 1966. Later, the 'North-West Project' to supply the Western Isles with colour television by 1975 required the construction of almost twenty relay stations north of Tobermory.

Before electricity was supplied to Skye, paraffin lamps and candles were the only forms of artificial light in most homes. Some hotels generated their own electricity. The Storr Lochs Hydroelectric Scheme completed in 1952 made electricity available to the whole of Skye. Other supplies now come to the island via underwater cables.

Fishing was one industry to benefit greatly from electrical supplies. Before it came to the island, ice was stored in the winter for use in packing fish caught later in the year. One of the last 'ice houses' to be used on a large scale in Britain was in Portree. It was owned by James Banks & Sons who took over the sea salmon fishings of Lord Macdonald of Sleat in 1943.

Fish from Banks & Sons was sent all over the country, as far as London, and required considerable amounts of ice to keep it fresh. The ice was obtained from a dam at Slugans about a mile out of Portree. In the winter, when the ice had reached one and a half inches thick, it was cut with a large blade like a scythe and transported to Portree where it was shovelled into a large chamber. When full, the door was sealed and covered with turf. Some years there was no ice at all, due to mild winters, and eventually an ice-making machine was installed inside the ice house.

Recently, construction began to link the Outer Hebrides to the National Grid. This has involved running an overhead line across Skye from near Broadford to Ardmore Point in Waternish. Conservationists objected saying that the poles and substations would be a blot on the landscape. The compromise was to supply wooden 'trident poles' instead of metal pylons, but the lines are still very obvious.

The homes of Skye's previously mighty clans are now tourist attractions. On inheriting the Clan Donald estates of Armadale in 1971, the present Chief of the Macdonalds, Lord Godfrey, had to sell off much of the land to pay death duties. The Clan Donald Lands Trust was founded to try to save some of the lands for the clan, and 18,000 acres were purchased, along with Armadale Castle. Part of the building became unsafe and was dismantled in 1980, leaving only the doorway and the lower part of the main stair.

The Storr

A portion of the castle buildings now houses the Clan Donald Centre, which is in part a museum dealing with the history of the Highland clans, mainly the Macdonalds. The centre attracts over 100,000 visitors a year, and also houses an extensive collection of books and archives for research into Highland history and tradition.

Lord and Lady Macdonald run a hotel in the eighteenth century Kinloch Lodge. The cuisine is famous and Lady Claire is a noted Scottish cookery writer. Lord Godfrey deals with the many enquiries sent to him about the clan – Clan Donald has over five million members. Although a Lord, Macdonald does not have a seat in the House of Lords. This is because he is actually an Irish peer. When the lordship was created, to reward the Macdonalds for not openly supporting the Jacobites, the clan

was still thought to be too powerful to be given a voice in the House of Lords. So the Macdonalds were given a lordship in the County of Antrim in Ireland.

Like the Clan Donald Centre, Dunvegan Castle is also one of Skye's foremost tourist attractions. The present chief is John, twenty-ninth Chief of MacLeod, and grandson of Dame Flora MacLeod of MacLeod. He is married to Melita Kolin, one of Bulgaria's best pianists, and they have established an annual Chamber Music Festival at the Castle.

Many of Skye's historical monuments have fallen into disrepair. Castles like Duntulm and Castle Moil have not been as lucky as Dunvegan and Armadale. The effort to preserve Castle Moil, for example, has been going on since the 1970s. Although Skye has no publicly owned museum, the plan is to look on the whole island as a landscape museum, and the island now has its first museums officer, Roger Miket.

One of a new breed of Skye landlord is Sir Iain Noble, a businessman and merchant banker. Sir Iain bought property on Skye when the Macdonald lands were being sold off, and experimented with estate management. Various businesses were established on the estate including a hotel, knitwear business, farms and a trading company. Sir Iain has also been active in attempts to revive the Gaelic culture, being involved in various schemes such as the provision of Gaelic roadsigns. In 1973 he established Sabhal Mor Ostaig – the Gaelic College – which among other courses, offers business studies in Gaelic. One of the college's aims is to encourage young people to stay in the Highlands and Islands.

It is estimated that half of Skye's population is Gaelic-speaking, but the number is decreasing. Most people in Skye would like to see Gaelic language and culture survive, according to a report of a working group for Comunn Na Ghaidlig, which has a ten year plan to spread Gaelic via the schools and 'Gaelic-medium' mother and toddler groups.

The Gaelic revival among the young people of Skye has been encouraged by Gaelic-speaking television programmes and the influence of folk and rock groups such as Runrig which write popular songs in Gaelic.

Rather than seeing Gaelic as detrimental to an island which strives to keep up with twentieth century advances, many are embracing the language as a symbol of pride in their island heritage. Gradually Skye, along with the Highlands in general, is shaking off the 'tartan trinkets' image foisted on it by early tourism. Hebridean goods such as clothing, crafts and food now enjoy an up-market image worldwide. Being an island is considered an asset in many respects.

This makes the issue of the proposed bridge link between Skye and the Mainland an even more emotive subject than it has been over the last fifty years. Recently, the debate even reached the *New York Times*, with the headline 'To Keep Peace on the Isle, Never Say Bridge'. Although a bridge will greatly speed up the crossing to Skye, many believe that the island will lose much of its appeal if getting there is not by boat. The anti-bridge lobby feel that psychologically Skye will no longer be an island.

Perhaps for some, a bridge symbolises Skye's demise as an island, the final amalgamation with mainland Scotland. There is no reason why this should be so – what makes Skye an island is not just a stretch of sea, it is an attitude, a sense of history and continuity, which will be preserved, bridge or no bridge.

Rainbow, Glen Sligachan

SKYE

How can't you see
The wilderness growing free
Time wounded and scarred
Stroking away the years
It's hard to believe
But memories are old ghosts
Mountains of black and gold
Sunsets falling over the moor
Take me there

You take your dream
And make life what you feel
Appearances lead to deceive
This drama so far from me
Destiny
On fates aching wings
Wild geese low over your shores
Hearts sailing over the trees
Take me there

Chi mi an t-eilean uaine
Tir nam beanntan arda
Ceò a'tuiteam tron a' ghleann
'Na shìneadh air do raointean

(copyright © C. Macdonald/R. Macdonald, Runrig)

SELECT BIBLIOGRAPHY

Bassin, Ethel, 1977, *The Old Songs of Skye: Frances Tolmie and her Circle*, London.

Bray, E., 1986, *The Discovery of the Hebrides: Voyagers to the Western Isles 1745–1883*, London.

Buchanan, Robert, 1873, *The Hebrid Islands*, London.

Campbell, J. G., 1900, *Superstitions of the Highlands and Islands of Scotland*, Glasgow.

Campbell, J. G., 1902, *Witchcraft and Second Sight in the Highlands and Islands of Scotland*, Glasgow.

Carmichael, Watson, J., ed., 1965, *Gaelic Songs of Mary MacLeod*, Edinburgh.

Cockburn, Lord H., 1888, *Circuit Journeys*, Edinburgh.

Collinson, Francis, 1966, *The Traditional and National Music of Scotland*, London.

Cooper, D., 1970, *Skye*, London.

Cooper, Derek, 1979, *Road to the Isles*, London.

Darling, F. Fraser, 1955, *West Highland Survey*, Oxford.

Donaldson, M. E. M., 1920, *Wanderings in the Western Highlands and Islands*, Paisley.

Grant, I. F., 1961, *Highland Folk Ways*, London.

Grimble, Ian, 1985, *Scottish Islands*, London.

Henshall, A. S., 1963 and 1972, *The Chambered Tombs of Scotland*, Edinburgh.

Highlands and Islands Development Board, 1986, *The Highlands and Islands: A Contemporary Account*, Inverness.

Humble, B. H., 1946, *The Songs of Skye*, Stirling.

Humble, B. H., 1952, *The Cuillin of Skye*, London.

Hunter, James and MacLean, Cailean, 1986, *Skye: The Island*, Edinburgh.

Johnson, Samuel, 1774, *A Journey to the Western Islands of Scotland*, London.

Knox, John, 1786, *Tour of the Highlands of Scotland and the Hebride Isles, A Report to the British Society for Extending the Fisheries 1786*, London.

Lamont, Revd D., (1913 edn), *Strath: in Isle of Skye*, Glasgow.

Lovell, J. P. B., 1977, *The British Isles through Geological Time*, London.

MacCowan, Roderick, 1902, *The Men of Skye*, Glasgow.

MacCulloch, J. A., 1905, *The Misty Isle of Skye*, Edinburgh.

MacCulloch, Rev John, 1824, *The Highlands and Western Isles of Scotland*, London.

MacGregor, Alasdair Alpin, 1926, *Over the Sea to Skye*, Edinburgh.

Mackay, John, 1914, *The Church in the Highlands*, London.

MacKenzie, Alexander, 1883, *The History of the Highland Clearances*, Inverness.

MacKenzie, William, 1933, *Skye Traditions, Reflections and Memories*, Culnacnoc.

MacLean, D. A., 1977, *Weather in North Skye*, Inverness.

MacLean, Fitzroy, 1970, *A Concise History of Scotland*, London.

MacLean, Sorley, 1986, 'Vale of Tears: A View of Highland History to 1886', in *As an Fhearann*, ed. Malcolm Maclean and Christopher Carrell, Edinburgh/ Stornoway/Glasgow.

MacLeod, Neil, 1924, *Clarsach an Doire*, Inverness.

Macneacail, Aonghas, 1986, *an seachnadh agus dàin eile*, Edinburgh.

MacPherson, G. W., 1982, *John Macpherson The 'Skye Martyr'*, Skye.

MacSween, Ann, 1985, 'The Brochs, Duns and Enclosures of Skye', *Northern Archaeology*, vols. 5 and 6.

MacSween, Ann, 1989, *Prehistoric Scotland*, London.

Martin Martin, 1703, *A Description of the Western Islands of Scotland*, London.

Matheson, William, 1970, *The Blind Harper*, Edinburgh.

Maxwell, Gavin, 1952, *Harpoon at a Venture*, London.

Miller, Hugh, 1856, *The Cruise of the Betsey*, Edinburgh.

Monro, Sir Donald, 1774, *Description of the Western Isles of Scotland called Hybrides*, Edinburgh.

Munro, Jean and Munro, R. W., 1986, *Acts of the Lords of the Isles 1336–1493*, Edinburgh.

Murray, C. W. and Birks, 1974, *The Botanist in Skye*, Portree.

Murray, Sarah, 1804, *A Companion and Useful Guide to the Beauties of Scotland*, London.

'Nauticus', 1884, *Nauticus in Scotland: a Tricycle Tour of 2,462 Miles*, London.

New Statistical Account of Scotland, 1845, vol. XIV, Edinburgh.

Nicolson, Alexander, 1930, *History of Skye*, Glasgow.

Pennant, Thomas, 1773, 1790, *A Tour of Scotland and a Voyage to the Hebrides*, London.

Prebble, John, 1963, *The Highland Clearances*, London.

Ritchie, Graham and Ritchie, Anna, 1981, *Scotland: Archaeology and Early History*, London.

Robertson, J. Graeme, 1988, *Skye Rural Land Use Survey*, Skye.

Royal Commission on the Ancient and Historical Monuments of Scotland, 1928, *An Inventory of the Ancient Monuments and Construction in the Outer Hebrides, Skye and the Small Isles*, Edinburgh.

Royal Commission on the Ancient and Historical Monuments of Scotland, 1985, *Exploring Scotland's Heritage: Argyll and the Western Isles*, Edinburgh.

Sanderson Taylor, Lucy, *These Quiet Stones*, Broadford, Skye.

Scott, Walter, 1982, *Northern Lights* (Scott's journal of his trip on the Lighthouse Boat), Hawick.

Shaw, Frances J., 1980, *The Northern and Western Islands of Scotland: Their Economy and Society in the Seventeenth Century*, Edinburgh.

Sillar, F. C. and Meyler, R., 1973, *Islands: Skye*, Newton Abbot.

Small, Allan, 1976, 'Norse Settlement in Skye', in *Les Vikings et leur Civilisation; problèmes actuels*, ed. R. Boyer, Paris.

Smith, Alexander, 1865, *A Summer in Skye*, London.

Smith, Revd Charles Lesingham, 1837, *Excursions through the Highlands and Isles of Scotland*, London.

Smout, T. C., 1969, *A History of the Scottish People 1560–1830*, Glasgow.

Swire, Otta, F., *Skye: The Island and its Legends*, Glasgow.

Statistical Account of Scotland, 1792–6, vols. II, III, IV, XVI, XVIII, 1792–6, vol. XIV, Edinburgh.

Steeple, E. W., Barlow, G., MacRobert, H. and Bell, J. H. B., 1948, *Island of Skye* (Scottish Mountaineering Club Guide), Edinburgh.

Storer, Ralph, 1989, *Skye: Walking, Scrambling and Exploring*, Newton Abbot.

Third Statistical Account of Scotland, 1985, vol. XVI, Edinburgh.

Thomson, Francis, 1984, *Crofting Years*, Barr.

Townshend, Rev Cauncy Hare, 1846, *A Descriptive Tour in Scotland*, London.

Walton, James, 1957, 'The Skye House', *Antiquity*, vol. 31, 155–162.

Whittow, J. B., 1977, *Geology and Scenery in Scotland*, Middlesex.

Yoxon, Paul and Yoxon, Grace M., 1987, *Guide to the Natural History of Skye*, Broadford, Skye.

Yoxon, Paul and Yoxon, Grace M., 1987, *Guide to the Geology of Skye*, Broadford, Skye.

Additional sources of information were *The Clarion of Skye*, *The Highlander* and *West Highland Free Press* newspapers, and the *Proceedings of the Society of Antiquaries of Scotland*.